ΛPPΛLΛCHIΛN
R E V I E W

VOL. 49, NO. 4
FALL 2021

TRADITION. DIVERSITY. CHANGE.

ESTABLISHED IN 1973
PUBLISHED QUARTERLY
by Berea College
www.appalachianreview.net

©2021 by Berea College. Vol. 49, No. 4 Fall 2021. All rights reserved. No part of this publication may be reproduced without the prior permission of *Appalachian Review*. Periodicals postage paid at Berea, Kentucky, and at additional mailing offices. ISSN# 03632318.

The short stories in this publication are works of fiction. Names, characters, places, and incidents are either the products of the authors' imaginations or are used fictitiously. Any resemblance to actual events, locales, or persons, living or dead, is entirely coincidental. The views expressed in the creative nonfiction herein are solely those of the authors. Electronic submissions only at www.appalachianreview.net. Distributed through a partnership between the University of North Carolina Press and Duke University Press. Basic subscription price: $30/year for individuals, $60/year for institutions. For subscription requests and inquiries, visit the magazine's website, email subscriptions@dukeupress.edu, or call 888-651-0122 (toll-free in the US and Canada) or 919-688-5134.

CONTENTS

CONTENTS

BOOK REVIEWS

COVER PHOTOGRAPH

Keeping Time by Lucian Alexe

EDITOR'S NOTE

JASON KYLE HOWARD

Here at Berea College, we are busy wrapping up the semester. A strange one it has been, fraught with the anxieties of being physically back in the classroom after an academic year of virtual learning and the heightened energy of hypervigilance against Covid-19 and its variants—of teaching, learning, and discussing from behind masks; of trying to read visual cues and sometimes failing miserably; of the hope that being vaccinated and boostered and following social distancing protocols will suffice.

As I write this, my introduction to creative writing students are completing a film analysis assignment. Revisions of short stories are coming due. They are preparing for our final class meeting, which will focus on the demands of the writing life and, more specifically, the necessity of making art a priority. They are reading the chilling words of Mary Oliver: "The most regretful people on earth are those who felt the call to creative work, who felt their own creative power restive and uprising, and gave to it neither power nor time."

They are invested in making the final push, but I have noticed that we are all—students and professors, them and me—more weary than usual. We are all in dire need of a break.

I'm looking forward to immersing myself in revising a manuscript, as well as reading for sheer pleasure. At the top of my reading stack is Sarah Gristwood's *The Tudors in Love,* Robert L. Jones's *The Prophets,* and Virginia Woolf's *Night and Day.* These are my companions for the grey, chilly days ahead—for nights with but "a smudge of moon", as William Kelley Woolfitt writes in an essay in this issue.

Woolfitt, who has made a name in Southern poetry, contributes three flash essays full of ache and lyricism. Seasoned author John Picard will transport you to film sets and fraught family dynamics in his story "The Exalted Present." Alongside Jemma, a neighbor and dog owner, you will face an unsettling dilemma in Dana Shavin's story "We're Very Sorry For Your Loss." Acclaimed poet Ron Houchin offers four poems exploring the fears of childhood. A trio of poems—two from Kelly Zanotti and one from Zachary Bartles—are steeped in the mysterious beauty of Ireland.

Karen Salyer McElmurray contributes a searching craft essay on memoir and family secrets. And in our interview, Jayne Moore Waldrop discusses her debut linked story collection *Drowned Town.*

As we move into the deepest part of autumn and stare at winter on the horizon, remain vigilant. Get boostered. With yet another variant on the horizon, take precautions. Mask up. Fight weariness with these tested remedies for the soul: free-write with no expectations, to just see what happens; visit a museum and lose yourself in the hidden worlds of a painting; spend an afternoon in nature, savoring the crunch of leaves beneath your boots; hold a treasured pet close for warmth and comfort. And always, keep company with some good words. ■

THE EXALTED
PRESENT

JOHN PICARD

L ate in life my father became a
Hollywood extra. Most people
when they retire take up gardening
or channel surfing. My father got an agent.
There were plenty of parts, it turned
out, for old men milling around Las
Vegas casinos, eating in crowded diners,
watching Christians being slaughtered
in the Coliseum. Over a ten-year span he

appeared in some twenty studio productions as well as several independents. My father was a shy man, a man of infinite reserve, and I can safely say he was the last one the family expected to pursue a film career, if that's what it was. He had never talked about how he would spend his retirement years, but then he never talked much period. He wasn't even a regular moviegoer, though neither was he an old fart who railed against the sex and violence in today's cinema. That would be Lincoln, my half-brother, who liked movies provid-ed they were made before the abolition of the Hays code, in 1968, when the movies, along with the rest of the country, began to go to hell.

Lincoln was at the hospital during my father's surgery for prostate and bladder cancer, meeting this crisis as he did all crises with a total lack of self-doubt. One of the few things I liked about my older brother was his willingness to indulge in the occasional cigarette. We walked to the edge of the hospital parking lot in the southern California sunshine, each of us puffing on a Camel Ultra Light.

"You know what this means, don't you?" Lincoln said. Only five-six, my brother had inherited from his mother, my stepmother, a roly-poly physique he did his best to control by eschewing sweets and most dairy products.

"What what means?"

"Now that he's wearing the bag he shouldn't be hanging around a movie set all day."

Lincoln had been apoplectic about my father's career since he debuted in *Lying In Wait,* popping up twenty minutes into the film pushing a grocery cart through a homeless shelter. I was tickled by it and gave Pop my full support. I'd come to see myself as my father's favorite, if only by default. We had the same laid back attitude toward most things. We sometimes exchanged looks when Lincoln went off on one of his America-Under-Siege rants. My father didn't have the same interest in the arts and culture that I had but he also didn't scorn them as the province of liberal elites. Before she died my stepmother admitted to me that Lincoln was jealous of me and my relationship with our father. I protested to her that there wasn't a whole lot to be jealous of. But Lincoln and I had always wanted as much of our silent father as we could get, and I couldn't help being pleased.

"What are you going to do, Linc?" I said. "You can't stop him. You know how stubborn he is."

"I know, Teddy, but things have changed. He's an eighty-two-year-old man with no bladder. He's going to have to empty that thing several times a day. Who's going to help him with that?"

"Lots of men wear the bag."

"Yeah, but they're not on fucking location in a city they don't know." Lincoln's disgust with cinematic profanity didn't stop him from using it in real life. He dropped his cigarette and ground it into the sidewalk with his size six shoe. "You know he's got this job, this shoot, whatever it's called, next month. I want you to go with him. You've got the time."

Lincoln didn't take my current vocation (freelance photographer with a closet-full of expensive camera equipment getting very little use at the moment) any more seriously than he did my other ones.

"I'd do it myself," he said, "but I'm backed up with cases." Lincoln was a very driven real estate attorney. "Will you do it?"

I wasn't about to tell Lincoln, but I'd already made up my mind to do it, having maxed out my Visa card weeks ago to cover my plane fare. I was looking forward to being on the set of Anton Starobinski, the directorial genius who made three or four of the all-time great films. But I wouldn't be there just as an observer of the great man. I had something I thought he might appreciate if I could just get it to him. It was no secret that Starobinski hadn't made an important film in years, not since *Rumours*. His mastery of mood and camera technique, his chemistry with his actors, were undiminished. The problem with his recent work was the story, the scripts. They were too light, too frivolous. Starobinski had lost his edge. You could still count on the Pole to turn out accomplished films, superb entertainments. But they lacked the wallop of his earlier work, the combination of moral seriousness and historical gravitas.

"If you really want me to go," I said, "I'll go."

"You'll have to fly. And you'll need to rent a car. How are your finances?"

I looked away.

"Why do I ask? I'll write you a check. Do you have a cell these days?"

"No." Things had been so tight lately that my phone service had been cut off.

"Get yourself a cell," Lincoln said. "I'll add it to the check. Because we need to stay in touch."

■ ■ ■

On a muggy evening in late June, Pop dozing in the seat beside me, I drove the rental car from the airport to a downtown hotel in the coastal city of Wilmington, North Carolina. Early the next morning—the temperature in the low eighties, the humidity almost as high—we walked to the roped-off street that had been taken over by the vast film crew.

I had been on a movie set before, but seldom one with movie stars and never with an auteur director. The second assistant director, a man in his thirties who introduced himself as Milosz, was responsible for directing the extras. Lithe, soft-spoken, intense, he huddled with each of them an hour or two before they were needed, blocked their scenes, then sent them off for more waiting.

"How you feeling, Pop?"

"Okay," my father said without glancing up from the sports page.

He looked frail to me, tentative in his movements, not one hundred percent post-surgery. Perhaps the secret of his longevity was that he didn't let anything like imperfect health or rubbing shoulders with celebrities distract him from his routines. As he did at the start of every day, he was reading the newspaper while partaking of the coffee and doughnuts (only one) provided gratis to cast and crew.

"I can call you when I'm done," he said. "You don't have to stay here."

Perhaps the secret of his longevity was that he didn't let anything like imperfect health or rubbing shoulders with celebrities distract him from his routines.

Was he being considerate, or did he prefer to be on his own? Impossible to tell. Either way, I knew that Lincoln, who was already calling me, would flip if he knew I wasn't at our father's side every second. Fortunately, Pop didn't seem to need any help with the bag and, as I suspected, Lincoln had exaggerated the necessity of a full-time nurse.

There were trucks and flood lights and sound booms up and down the street. Three trailers were parked at the end of the block, one each for the two stars of the film, the other for the director. Linda Logan had yet to appear. Her contract stipulated that none of the so-called "subordinate cast and crew"—laborers, bit players, extras—was allowed to approach her or even look at her. There were young people with clipboards and cups of coffee dashing about self-importantly, no doubt recent graduates of the country's best film schools. All the females among them seemed to be blonde with tiny waists and long legs. Then there was Starobinski, a balding, energetic little man in khakis and a polo shirt looking younger than his seventy-plus years. Three or four assistants followed him wherever he went. He was mesmerizing; I couldn't take my eyes off him. If he'd had Linda Logan's contract I would have already been kicked off the set. I watched him turn to the second assistant director. Rising on his toes, he put the younger, taller man in a loose headlock and drew him aside for a tête-à-tête.

"Looks like Milosz is in good with the director," I said to Pop. "That's his son."

■ ■ ■

I had been trying to write a salable, full-length screenplay for years, one of several endeavors—mystery writer, venture capitalist, cordon bleu chef, editor of a Harry Potter webzine— that hadn't quite panned out. Without getting too mystical about it, I'd always felt there was something special, something a touch glamorous and out of the ordinary, I was fated to do—if I could only discover what that was. In the past I'd never gotten beyond thirty or forty pages on any screenplay with subjects ranging from Marilyn Monroe to Sacco and Vanzetti. What I needed, it so happened, was a certain kind of pressure, a deadline. When I learned six weeks before his surgery that Pop would be breathing the rarefied air of Anton Starobinski, I'd applied myself to my screenwriting as never before. After doing some research, the story, the words, came to me almost as fast as they do in Hollywood movies where the writer, previously blocked, bangs out non-stop sentences with closeups of his blinding-fast fingers, cigarette butts overflowing the ashtray, unblinking eyes watching the miracle unfold, triumphal music rising to a crescendo. Rocky at the keyboard.

But the longer I was on Starobinski's set the more I felt my confidence wane. You can't overstate how busy a movie director is and I was finding it harder and harder to imagine rushing up to Starobinski between takes and thrusting my ninety-five pages at him. I decided on a more roundabout route.

On the third day of the shoot the extras were being filmed in a Greek restaurant, sitting in booths with plates of spanakopita and souvlaki in front of them. My father sat across from a woman roughly his age. It was a simple scene, a scene, like so many, with only an even chance of surviving the editing process, and with just extras in it, less than that. I think I knew what Pop got out of this kind of work—traveling, the open air, a feeling of independence—but what the others derived from it, men and women in middle age and younger, people in their prime, was harder to fathom. I'd learned that many of them had once been aspiring actors who were trying to make a living out of extra work, who'd given up on doing any real acting, who'd settled, in other words. I imagined they told themselves that one day they'd be plucked from the horde of anonymous extras and given a speaking part, the first step toward stardom, even though that never happened and they had to know it never happened. Extras didn't even receive screen credit. Their job was to blend in, to go virtually unperceived, appearing for fractions of seconds on the cinematic periphery. I found them somewhat depressing, these also-rans who, sad to say, were no more impactful in a movie than they were in life.

Milosz announced a fifteen-minute break. When I hurried over he was sitting in a corner of the restaurant talking to one of his assistants.

"Excuse me," I said. "I don't mean to interrupt, but I wonder if I could ask you a favor."

Milosz reared back and regarded me quizzically. "Oh. Tony's friend."

"Son, actually."

"What kind of favor?"

"I wonder if you could see that your father gets this."

He glanced at the stack of paper with a rubber band around it. "Don't tell me. A screenplay."

"I thought maybe you could pass it along. At your convenience, of course."

"He won't read it."

"He might if he knows what it's about."

"Which is?"

"The camps."

"Ah," Milosz said. "That's your angle."

It was well known that members of Starobinski's family had perished in the Sobibor death camp. For decades, for as long as he had been making movies, there had been speculation that the director was planning to make his Holocaust film.

"It's not an angle," I said. "I just thought it might be something your father would naturally be interested in. This isn't *Schindler's List.* There's no sappy ending. It's about people in conditions where the only thing that matters is survival. Where it's every man for himself." I was tempted to add that the movie his father was currently making, a seaside rom-com that risked comparisons to the beach party movies of the American fifties and sixties, was unworthy of the great man's talents, but I refrained. Continuing with my pitch, "This might not be the exact screenplay for him, but I think it's the sort of serious examination of the extremes of the human condition he's been looking for."

Milosz was staring up at me. "The camps, huh?"

"Yes."

"All right."

"Thanks," I said and thrust my manuscript at him before he could change his mind, adding, "You can glance at it yourself if the subject interests you." It struck me that Milosz wouldn't remain a second assistant director forever, that he must have ambitions of his own.

■ ■ ■

Over the following days Pop appeared in a variety of little scenes, both interior and exterior. Hours passed between set-ups. Bored silly, I set my sights on Danielle, the script supervisor on the picture. I liked her confident air and the little prance in her athletic stride. Whenever she had a break I sidled over, but I wasn't getting anywhere, not even when I engaged her in the favorite pastime on any movie set, gossiping about the cast and crew. The best I could do was get her to admit she didn't like Milosz. "He's kind of a prick."

Meanwhile, I let myself imagine Starobinski stealing precious moments from his heavy workload to pour over the pages that would reestablish his reputation as one of the world's great filmmakers, and do it with the movie he'd wanted to make his entire life.

"Hey Pop. You know how I've always wanted to write a screenplay. Well, I did it. I wrote one. And Starobinski has it. I gave it to him four days ago."

I had vowed not to tell anyone in order to spare myself the embarrassment when the director returned the manuscript without a word via Milosz or some flunky. I wouldn't have either, told anyone, if I hadn't found the nerve to ask Milosz outright whether he'd done what I requested—without being aggressive or too needy about it—and he had nodded that yes, he had given his father my screenplay. In the same conversation he urged me to join Pop in a crowd scene to be filmed in a local park, ("I'll put you on the payroll"), but I told him I wasn't interested.

"Four days he's had it," I said to my father. "I can't help thinking that means something."

"What time you got?"

"Eleven-thirty."

"Better be getting over to that coffee place." Milosz was shooting that afternoon outside a Starbucks. It was sad to think Starobinski had sunk to product placement.

I said, "Even if he decides not to do it, which he won't, of course, he may be able to point me in the right direction professionally. Anyway, Starobinski's not going to do my screenplay. I know that. The more important thing is I finished it, right?"

"Right," he said. Then, after a pause, he spoke the words, or words to the effect, I'd been hoping to hear all along: "Good for you."

■ ■ ■

Another tedious day of waiting around in steamy weather, this time at the beach. Two hours passed without anything happening and, after checking in with Pop, who had fallen asleep under a cabana, I wandered off, hoping to catch Starobinski in action. He was working two hundred yards down the beach, a tracking shot of Linda Logan and Cal Lambert strolling the shore. Arriving between takes, I found

18

Danielle sitting under a beach umbrella and making notes on a legal pad.

"How's it going here?" I said.

"Not good. The light sucks."

"Where's the man?"

"He broke for lunch."

"I wanted to ask you. Have you seen him reading anything?"

"You mean like a book?"

"Anything."

"I don't think Anton has much time for reading."

"The reason I ask....he happens to have one of my screenplays."

She stopped what she was doing and, moving aside a length of dark blonde hair, looked up at me. "You're a writer?"

"Yeah."

"He actually said he'd look at your screenplay?"

"Once he knew what it was about he did."

"What's it about?"

She stopped what she was doing and, moving aside a length of blonde hair, looked up at me. "You're a writer?"

I told her.

"The long-awaited Holocaust movie," she said.

"Exactly. I feel honored he's even considering it."

"You never know," Danielle said. "Anton likes to do the unexpected. *Journey of No Return* was adapted from that English novelist no one ever heard of."

"I'd hadn't thought of that." I had, of course. I'd thought of little else. "Hey," I said, "speaking of lunch, I know you're busy but how would you like to grab a bite? There's a tiki bar right over these dunes."

She shrugged. "Okay."

Over crab cakes and white wine we talked about our careers. She admitted to the unrealistic hope of directing her first feature film before she turned thirty (her hero was actress-cum-director Ida Lupino), but she would be content to pay her dues as an assistant director with any major studio or respectable independent.

"What about you?" she said. "What other screenplays have you written?" I could tell from her concentrated gaze and the tilt of her pretty head, that she was genuinely intrigued by this older—but not yet old—man who had somehow gotten the attention of the God-like director. A few flakes of stardust had drifted down and stuck to me. I mentioned a few of my other creative efforts without going into detail. My bona fides established, I steered the conversation on to other topics: my two exes, her one.

I paid the bill with Lincoln's money, leaving a large tip Danielle couldn't fail to notice.

I almost took her hand as we were walking back to the beach.

"Good luck with your screenplay," she said as we crested the dune that brought the ocean into view. "Oh, look."

Down the beach a rotating red light was sweeping the set.

"Is that an ambulance?" Danielle said.

I started running.

■ ■ ■

At the hospital I used my new cell to call Lincoln. There was no answer and I left a message. I was standing in the hospital parking lot, smoking a cigarette, when the phone rang.

"How's he doing?"

"Not too bad," I said. "It wasn't a major stroke. His speech is a little slurred, and he can't do much with his left arm, but the doctor said Pop would make a complete recovery."

"When are they going to release him?"

"A couple of days. After that he'll need to go to a nursing facility for rehabilitation."

"I'll let you arrange that. I knew something like this would happen. Goddamn movie bullshit."

"Nothing's happened, Linc. He's going to be fine."

"Keep me posted."

I returned to Pop's room and explained to him that he was going to have to be moved in a few days to a rehabilitation center in either Raleigh or Greenville. "But don't worry, Pop. I'll be with you all the way."

He tried to speak, but the slackness on one side of his mouth made it difficult to enunciate. A minute later he was asleep.

My cell rang only minutes after I returned to my hotel room. It was Milosz. He asked me about Pop, then said, "The old man wants to talk to you. I'll get back to you when he's free."

"Thanks, man. Thanks a lot."

"Tell Tony we're thinking about him."

"I will. Thanks, again."

I tried to take a nap but was I too wound up. I went looking for Danielle and learned that filming had been suspended due to the weather and that some of the crew had headed into town. I found them at Circa 1922, a swanky bar on North Front Street, gathered around a long table drinking chocolate martinis. After I assured everyone that Pop was on the mend, I ordered one for myself. Over time, as more and more of the crew peeled away, I got close enough to Danielle to whisper my news.

"You're kidding?" she said.

"Nope."

"That's fantastic. When?"

"Soon, I think."

"That's fantastic," she repeated and squeezed my hand. We ordered another drink; real martinis this time. Danielle studied me over the rim of her glass, her blue-grey eyes holding the same fledgling admiration I'd noted earlier. It was more intoxicating than any amount of alcohol, a taste of what it must be like to live in the exalted present, in that heightened reality enjoyed by the elites of the world and those lucky enough to bask in their golden glow. While most people lived obscure lives of minor consequence, these special few thrived on the big stage, members of the planet's most exclusive club. If you doubted it, try getting Tom Cruise on the phone.

We left the bar at closing, Danielle charging the bill to the studio. It was drizzling, a touch of unseasonable coolness in the air. A mist had settled in, giving the street lamps and car headlights a gauzy radiance. I didn't have to ask where we were going.

We rode the elevator to the fourth floor of Danielle's hotel. We had a nightcap, then lay on top of one of the two queen beds and made out. That was as far it went, but there was a promise in it, a future. I fell quickly to sleep after Danielle returned from the bathroom and slipped into the other bed.

I awoke at ten and dashed off a short note to Danielle who was still asleep, then practically ran down the sidewalk to the rental and sped to the hospital. To my amazement I found Lincoln sitting at our father's bedside. Jumping up, he grabbed my elbow and led me down the corridor.

"I've been calling you for hours," he said. "What happened to your phone, Teddy?"

"I turned it off, I guess. What are you doing here?"

"Pop called me. Well, one of the nurses did. I took the red eye. Where the hell have you been?"

"I had something I had to do."

"Yeah? What's her name?"

I said nothing.

Lincoln shook his head at me. "Pop told me what happened. He said the last thing he remembered was looking for a bathroom. Someone found him lying on a foot bridge, covered with urine. Why weren't you with him? Where were you, for Chrissake?"

"Back off, Linc."

"They're discharging him first thing tomorrow. I'll be driving him to this rehab place in Raleigh."

"I already told him I'd do that."

"He wants me to do it."

"Then you must have bullied him."

I walked past Lincoln and back into the room. Pop's eyelids were drooping, but he was conscious. He could hear me as I made my apology, explaining, "I've been in this crazy state since I heard from Starobinski. That's right, Pop. He wants to see me."

"What are you talking about?" Lincoln said.

"You wouldn't understand."

"Can't you see he's exhausted? Stop pestering him."

"Fuck you."

"Fuck you."

"Listen, Pop. I'll make this up to you. I promise. Hang in there."

■ ■ ■

The next day I stuck close to Milosz who was working outside a boarded-up movie theater in the middle of downtown. He could see my frustration.

"Relax," Milosz said. "He'll get to you. Say, how'd you like to be in this shot coming up. All you have to do is exit the theater with the others. You don't even have to change clothes."

"No thanks," I said.

Only minutes after completing the scene, he waved me over. "I just got off the phone with the old man." Milosz nodded.

I felt my heart jump.

We walked around the block where the director was in an intense conversation with Linda Logan. After what seemed an hour but was probably only a few minutes, the actress touched the director's arm, kissed him lightly on the cheek, then allowed her personal assistant to lead her away.

Milosz brought me over to his father and formally introduced us.

I was sitting in a straight back chair, ankle crossed over knee. The director stood so close I could see a line of sweat on his upper lip.

"Come with me," Starobinski said in his accented English. I tried to keep up with his short, vigorous strides. I was literally walking in the great man's footsteps as he moved swiftly up the stairs and into his trailer. He picked my screenplay off a table and held it in his mottled hands. His wireless glasses were low on his long, thin nose.

"You know much about the Holocaust, yes?"

"I've delved fairly deeply into the Holocaust literature," I said.

"Levi, Kuznetsk, Wiesel...Such like?"

"Exactly."

"You are student of the Holocaust."

"Yes."

"Did you think I was not?"

"I'm sorry?"

I was sitting in a straight back chair, ankle crossed over knee. The director stood so close I could see a line of sweat on his upper lip. He said, "Did you think I would not recognize characters from the most famous of Holocaust books?"

"I don't follow."

"Do you have so little respect for victims of the Holocaust that you steal all they have left—the memory of their suffering."

"I don't know what you mean."

"Sons abusing fathers. That is your theme. Sons abusing fathers except for your Moshe and your Jacob. But even Moshe wishes his father dead and for that he feels terrible guilt." Starobinski opened the screenplay, flipped the pages. He read aloud, "'There are no fathers, no brothers, no friends. Everyone lives and dies for himself alone here.' A kapo says in *Night*. A prisoner says the same in your writing. Moshe is made to give up his gold tooth by a guard who digs it out with a fork. A spoon in *Night*. All the way through. Same thing."

"I consulted several of the better known sources about the Shoah and some of that may have gotten into the finished product."

"Shoah. Is that to impress me? You did not consult. You stole."

"I took some liberties, I admit, but the world's been waiting a long time for Starobinski's Holocaust movie."

"You know better than Starobinski what films he should make."

"Of course not. I just mean—"

"Get out. Go," he said. "And take this—what is it you Americans call it?—*rip-off*." He dropped the screenplay in my lap.

■ ■ ■

I didn't know what to do with myself except buy a fifth of Jim Beam and drink enough of it to numb the disappointment and humiliation. Even so, I burst into tears before sinking into a dead, dreamless sleep. In the morning, hungover, I called the number Lincoln had given me for the rehab center in Raleigh.

Lincoln answered.

"How's Pop doing?" I asked.

"Fine. Now."

"Can you put him on?"

"He isn't doing much talking."

"Can you just put him on, Linc? Can you do that for me?... Pop? You there?"

I heard a low rumble.

"Starobinski passed on my screenplay. No big surprise, of course, but that doesn't mean it feels good."

There was only silence. What had I expected?

"I love you, Pop," I said.

Then Lincoln was back on. "You still in Wilmington?"

"I can be there in a few hours."

"Don't bother. We're flying out later today. I'm taking him home. Where he goddamn belongs."

After showering, I went looking for Danielle. At first I thought she was upset with me for barging in on her conversation with the boom operator. I couldn't think of any other reason for her curt response to my invitation to lunch. "Maybe. Probably not." Of course, I thought, walking away, she'd heard. News travels fast on a movie set and word had reached her about my disgrace. I couldn't get off the set fast enough. But before I reached the rental someone called my name.

It was Milosz coming toward me, clipboard in hand. "Are you sure I can't interest you in some work?" he said. "Nonunion extras earn ninety dollars a day. I have this big beach scene coming up and I need all the bodies I can get. Wardrobe can fit you with a bathing suit."

"I'm not very popular on the set right now," I said.

"No one cares about that. He was pretty rough on you, huh?"

"He accused me of plagiarism."

"The memory of the Holocaust is sacred to my father. He's afraid he can't do it justice. You just reminded him of it. Anyway, you won't be dealing with the old man. You'll be dealing with me."

"Ninety dollars, you said?"

An hour later I was among the throng lying on beach towels, throwing freebies, floating in the ocean.

Just beyond the breaking waves, I bobbed up and down with two young girls sitting in rubber innertubes, and half a dozen adults of various ages who, like myself, were straddling beach mattresses.

"Ready?" Milosz shouted through his bullhorn from the shore.

As instructed, I stretched out and lay face down on the mattress.

"Action!"

I dangled my arms over the sides, I lowered my feet into the water, drifting with the current. ■

FIRST BELIEF

Religion may have begun with fear of thunder
and lightning, in conflict with the sanctity of sleep.

The *Now-I-lay-me-down* charm worn off,
I was bungeed out of dream into the strobe light

of a summer night. I toddled past the high bed
where my parents lay facing south like Mount Rushmore,

and I was quiet as long as paramount need allowed.
I believed in the protection of sheets. Ghosts

under their covers were there not for my benefit.
I couldn't withstand the presence of such absence,

their two faces of shadow. I whimpered past,
back to the room of black and white convulsion.

No teddy bear, no story book relieved what I'd learned
of the world and the aloneness of fear. Beyond

my window, where it all went on, a streetlamp kept
preaching steady light. Not in my head

then, but now contrasts were what I feared,
no distance between the stark flash, the slow roll.

RON HOUCHIN

GETTING READY FOR CHURCH

Before the starched white shirt
and the oxblood polished shoes,
I suit up my head, hair slicked back
with the beliefs of my grandparents;

starting a fire on Sunday causes
your face to appear in the moon
and sitting quietly with feet up
during a thunderstorm shows
you fear of God's power.

Gospel music on the radio
for the ride to worship, then waiting
on a wooden pew for the erratic magic
of the universe, I stared at the feathers
in paintings speaking to that part

of my head wants to fly, holding my early
question of why there's a spire so tall
over the door. When the reverend appears,
I'm ready to give up my pocket change
to get away with the day.

RON HOUCHIN

DREAM OF ELEPHANTS

Tonight they stand outside windows, like boulders
set on tables with pillars for legs so big any one
could carry the world. They're grey in the blackness,
as if held-light dilutes their once-dark camouflage.
When I look at one, the others fill the corners of my eyes.
I run outside and bawl, standing among them,
We call you elephant because you are elevated, yet
heavy with phantasy we place on your backs like rajas.

Back inside, I watch them slim the space between trees.
My breath comes back at me windowpane to windowpane
as I repeat the three syllables to squares of glass so each
will know the name of the thing it sees, the being that night
must rub around. I am so young in my dream
I believe everything it has to say.

RON HOUCHIN

SLEEPING WITH A LIGHT ON

the room grows soft around its edges
and the edges of things. The clutter

of the side table becomes hushed as if clock,
cell phone, and car keys have changed

their demeanor to a growing thing.
My eyes twinkle with Spanish moss,

the room shifting southern and relaxed.
In the low rays of the lamp,

I see the fatigue of things, their vulnerability.
We are all just waiting for the same asteroid.

RON HOUCHIN

APPROXIMATION #62

What mystery we witnessed
while living in the low country.

We once found a tabby dead in the street
and buried her in the field behind our house.
Three days later, she climbed in through an open window.
The field: nothing but an empty grave.

Another time we saw a woman with silver hair
waltzing naked across our porch.
She wailed *Reset! Reset! Reset!*
until somoeone (not us) called the police.

The strangest was the Cadillac with no driver
that once circled our street for hours
while a blood moon hung
like an iced plum in the sky.

Forgive this approximation.

What I really want to say is this:
I am thinking tonight of you.
You told me a world without resurrections
isn't worth the story you'd give it.

Back then I rolled my eyes.

DAN LEACH

A IS FOR
ARK
POPULATION

WILLIAM KELLEY WOOLFITT

I am at the aquarium in Chattanooga with my older son, holding his hand as we descend the walkways that zigzag down the Secret Reef. He's two-and-a-half, might be language-delayed. He's not saying much. Every so often, a word. Or he makes a sound. Today, he reaches his hand toward rippling water, green sea turtle, thousands of bright fish. So much to take in. I can call what I see in him awe. Inside the observation bubble of the Undersea

Cavern, we sprawl on our backs, look up at the reef, the bellies of sandbar sharks. Next, we will go searching for the tanks of endangered topminnows and laurel dace, relocated here after severe drought dried up their shoestring creeks on the Barrens Plateau and Cumberland Plateau. "Fish," my son says. "Fish swim," I say, give him an encouraging look, hope he will say more, will go on. He looks at me, turns his head, peers at something I can't see.

■ ■ ■

Reef. Formerly riff. A riff or ridge of rocks, *Dampier's Voyages* (1681). Icelandic. *rif,* a reef in the sea; cf. *rifa,* a rift, rent, fissure. See Rift, Rive.

■ ■ ■

Dace, a Dart; also, a Dare fish; so called from its darting motion.

■ ■ ■

At bedtime, I read to both my sons. I read *The Underwater Alphabet Book.* I say, "A is for angelfish." The baby runs his hand over the page, looking for a flap to lift. He loves all things peekaboo. I read, "There are enough different kinds of angelfish for someone to write an Angelfish Alphabet Book." My older son says, "More." Maybe he means that there are more wonders in the world than we know; maybe he's asking for another book. I read *Mike Mulligan and His Steam Shovel.* He's fascinated by bulldozers, backhoes, loaders. We call them diggers. I read, "Mary Ann could dig as much in a day as a hundred men could in a week." I read, "Mary Ann lowered the hills and straightened the curves to make the long highways."

After I tuck my sons in, I surf the web. I read about excavators and mountaintop removal, marine life and rising ocean temperatures on Wikipedia and Twitter. I read that a successor to the steam shovel was the Marion 5960-M, a multi-ton stripping shovel that tore out veins of coal at the River Queen Surface Mine in Muhlenberg County, Kentucky. I scroll until I'm worried, my pulse quickens, something is squeezing me. I read until I learn about this:

■ ■ ■

Once, there was an amber forest humming in the Pacific Ocean, teeming with abalones—snails with flat oval shells, wide mouths, a series of breathing holes. Near rocky reefs and crags, two gold-brown seaweeds, giant Pacific kelp and bull kelp, grew as many as ten inches a day. These kelps rippled from holdfasts that rooted them, rippled up, up, up to canopy-mats floating on gas bladders. Some people called them the sequoias of the sea. The kelp-fronds would *rise and fold and unfold,* providing habitat for sheepsheads, opal eyes, keyhole limpets, sea cucumbers and long-spined purple urchins. Spider crabs grazed there, and turban snails, sea stars, and abalones.

■ ■ ■

Kelp, *n.* 1. Large, cold-water seaweed. 2. The ashes left from the burning of seaweed, used for making soap and glass.

■ ■ ■

Abalone: Rumsen (Southern Ohlone) aūlun n. red abalone, e.g., *Harper's Mag.* (1861): the coast Indians carry on a small trade with the Indians of the mountains, dried abalone in exchange for berries and acorns.

■ ■ ■

Since commercial harvesting began, the abalone have been imperiled. In 1881, one magazine claimed that *the shell business has been extensive for four years, but the abalone may soon become exterminated.* In 1913, reporting on the abalone harvest in California, James Edwards describes *a diver sending the net up, filled with about fifty green and corrugated abalones, every six or seven minutes.* In 1914, Nellie Sanchez said that *iridescent abalone shells once covered the beaches with a glittering carpet. With our usual easy-going American negligence, we have permitted these creatures, valuable for their edible meat as well as for their exquisitely colored shells, to be nearly destroyed.*

■ ■ ■

Riff, *n.* A repeated phrase; an improvisation, variation, or commentary on a theme.

■ ■ ■

Then there was the Blob—a patch of too-warm water in the Pacific, two thousand miles long. Although anchovies and krill became scarce, although sea lions, auklets, and many creatures starved, urchins thrived. California's kelp forest is overrun with urchins now, chewed to nubs, frondless, a ravaged mess. Scaling the urchin-stripped stalks, the few abalones find almost no food.

■ ■ ■

Leah Mata, a Chumash artist, says *it's hard to locate mallard ducks, to find abalones and clams.* The saltmarshes are too dry for mallards. Mata makes feather dance belts, fishhooks and regalia from shells she buys in flea markets.

■ ■ ■

The laurel dace—yellow-finned, orange-bellied—could have died out when drought thinned and fragmented the creeks they lived in, stranded the last survivors in meager puddles *that dotted the dense blanket of fallen leaves covering the creekbeds.* Conservationists caught eighteen laurel dace with seine nets, transported them to the Chattanooga aquarium, now maintain them as an ark population.

■ ■ ■

In a glass niche, the rescued Barrens topminnows flash through the strands of yarn mops.

■ ■ ■

I can keep believing that if he says one word, he will say one more. That his delay will not diminish him. I can borrow a creed from what the frog-man said when he refused the witch: I'm going to stand by a world where one more is possible.

■ ■ ■

Another name for abalone is *sea ear.*

■ ■ ■

Tonight, one son sleeps. One son chatters for a while, and then he sleeps too. My wife is working the night shift at a psychiatric hospital. Our house is moon-silvered, a deep ocean, the holdfast of a dreaming family. My life depends on theirs. We repeat. We are connected. There's laurel dace in me, abalone in me, amber seaweed. I'm an ear for faint cries, for bits of story. ■

J IS FOR
JEWELWEED

WILLIAM KELLEY WOOLFITT

Aphasia

I thought that there would be a worse day, that my grandmother would live long enough not to speak to any of us at all.

Bird Feeder

When the feeders she had hung in the peach trees were too far, she left little piles of millet and sunflower seed on the porch rails.

Cows

For forty years, she and my grandfather worked the farm on Pea Ridge. In the morning, she would *walk out to see the cows*. For fifteen years, she gardened alone.

Dark-eyed juncos

She also called them snowbirds, and fed the big flocks that visited in winter, and heard its two songs, metallic trill and low warble.

Eye

The old pond in her woods is shrinking, reverting to an eye: *where an underground spring surfaces, soaks dry ground, gives us a glimpse of all that happens outside human vision.*

Firstborn

My son was born when she was almost ninety. He was language-delayed while she was becoming quiet, less sure of her words. Both of them slow to talk. I didn't know what to say.

Garden

In her journal, she wrote: *Haven't taken good care of it. The deer & bean beetles & green tomato worms have been competing—may not plant as much next year (God willing).*

Hunting Season

Why she couldn't walk in the woods in December. She wrote: *I saw nine deer run across the meadow, with a hunter shooting. I was glad he missed. I'm for the deer.*

I'll Fly Away

an historical drama on NBC, one of her favorite programs, we watched together. I learned about the Civil Rights Movement when Lily Harper tried to vote.

Joe froggers

molasses cookies she made at Christmas. Named for Black Joe, a tavern keeper, son of a slave mother, a Wampanoag father. Sailors took joe froggers to sea because they were durable.

Knowledge

In her last year, she recognized her family, learned new things, interacted with her environment, was still trying to communicate. She loved phone calls, hymns, dogs, and great-grandchildren.

Lea Meadow

what she called one part of her farm. Lea is an Old English word that means *open, untilled land; grassy plain; stretch of level fields.*

Morels

mushrooms she gathered. In Silesia, an old woman who shouldn't have gone out at night was torn up by the Devil. Wherever a piece of her fell, there grew another morel.

Nursing bucket

She wrote: *February 27. Sunny, cold, 20's. A new calf this morning—a bull, all black. I went down and held the bucket for him. He was cold and couldn't get started nursing his mother.*

O Beulah Land

I imagine her singing into the tape recorder: *I've reached the land of corn and wine. All my night has passed away.*

Peace

She opposed pro-war presidents, the 88,000 tons of bombs dropped on Iraq, the brutal deaths of civilians who were in the wrong air raid shelter, the wrong neighborhood.

Quick-in-the-hand

Also called touch-me-not, jewelweed. In West Virginia, some people boil it, eat it with salt and butter, or use it to treat poison ivy. Kathryn Nuernberger calls it *one of those plants that will be with us until the end of the world.*

Rock Garden

She wrote: *So far we've gotten new potatoes, snap peas, onions, radishes, lettuce—from the rock garden. A miracle. It's full of rocks, despite me removing so many from there.*

St. Mary's

In 1945, she joined the Cadet Nurses Corp, went to St. Mary's Hospital at Clarksburg for her training. The nuns taught her to work in the surgery, nursery, supply room.

Trillium

In the spring, she looked for jewelweed and trilliums in the woods. Trilliums favor *cold deep ravines along runs. Mountain superstition says if a woman picks a white trillium, it will rain.*

Unreal

My grandfather died of lymphoma when she was seventy-one. She wrote: *everything seemed to be happening to someone else—so unreal to me.*

Vascular

Maybe the brain wasn't getting enough blood, maybe high blood pressure. Confusion, memory problems, slow or unsteady gait.

White Dog

a movie she liked. After his wife dies, Sam Peek, a pecan farmer, sees a dog that only he can see. His grown children think he's senile.

X-ray

She fell and broke five ribs at the end of September.

Yoga

She was the first person I knew who did yoga as exercise, who recycled household trash, who gave money to charities, worked crossword puzzles, searched the dictionary for the right word.

Z words

She used obscure Z words for strategic maneuvers in Scrabble, recited *whose woods these are I think I know,* sometimes identified herself in voice messages as *guess who.* ∎

O IS FOR
ORIGIN

WILLIAM KELLEY WOOLFITT

I can begin here: remembering my grandparents on icy winter nights. When I see glimmers in the dark, bits of light, I think of their farm on Pea Ridge in Barbour County. I can imagine a smudge of moon, my grandfather tracking the snow as he walked over the knob, around the new pond, down into the hickory woods where his shadow mixed with tree-shadows and you couldn't tell one from the other.

When snow drifts flanked their house, my grandfather made popcorn in a skillet with bacon grease. In the basement, my grandmother stirred the red coals in the smoldering furnace.

If it were Christmas Eve, she would light the magi candle and offer me molasses cookies; my grandfather would play his guitar and sing "Mamas Don't Let Your Babies Grow Up to Be Cowboys." Outside, the snow would be coming down fast, sure to stick to sassafras and sumac, the lip of the trough, the cow bones scattered through the woods. Ice would seal the old pond that shrank each year. I can imagine my finger or nose freezing to chrome letters on the spare-parts truck, and icicles bearding the pine trees. Soon, the snow would cover my grandfather's tracks, blanket their farm, making it unfamiliar, a story written over.

■ ■ ■

In the summer when I was thirteen, I stayed with them during hay season. My grandfather listened to the weather radio, the meteorological feed from Backbone Mountain, making sure there was little chance of rain. My grandmother and I were playing five hundred rummy in the kitchen, and he scowled at us. He told me, *Go put your long pants on.* His way of saying he wanted me to work with him outside.

In the meadows, I stepped around splats of manure; I stomped on a puffball, and it coughed up its rich brown dust. I was too scrawny to lift the bales onto the flatbed truck, but I helped my grandfather and my uncle by rolling the bales, grouping them together. Grasshoppers sprung from the hay stubble. My skin was scratched by stems, timothy heads, the rough twine.

We unloaded and stacked the bales in the stuffy hayshed that smelled like warm grass. I saw the mud nests of swallows, light that spilled between cracks in the wall-boards. My grandfather kept tractor-parts there, and come-alongs, buckets, pans of axle grease.

Later, I took a bath. My grandmother gave me aloe for the scratches on my neck and arms. When we all sat down for supper, my grandfather was tired from hay work, from pouring himself out. My grandmother had cooked for us sirloin tips from their butchered steer, onions from their garden, and morels she picked under a dying tulip tree.

■ ■ ■

And then my grandfather was diagnosed with lymphoma, and it riddled, wasted, and thinned all that he was. He gave up his chainsaw and rototiller. He became housebound, and sat by the window in his soft recliner, and counted dark-eyed snowbirds on the telephone wire.

He had chemo, remission, relapse. Finally, my grandmother insisted that his oncologists say it to her plain. Say the truth about him she had made life with, him she had known fifty years, had known field after field cut and raked and cured, jar upon jar of peppers and applesauce and pickles, the chest freezer full of beef and blackberries in tubs, and all the Hereford calves.

He has a few weeks left. We can make him comfortable.

She moved him home, the house he had built for them. She put the railed bed in the living room with its plenty of windows, tilted it so he would see family pictures on the mantel, and the dirt road. And see the maple and peach trees, the nearest meadow, and the mockingbird, and their cows. If he lifted his head, opened his eyes. He was all bone, light as a bag of hay.

My grandmother said, *He was always strong, always in charge, and very positive.*

46

Now, he grew anxious if she went outside. He wanted her near. She stopped tending the garden. She stayed by him, and tucked his sheets, and dabbed his brow, and brought ice she had beaten to slivers, and held the cold shards to his lips.

■ ■ ■

While he rested in the next room, my grandmother and I ate in the kitchen.

Tell me about how you met him, I said. I thought it was a story that she liked to tell.

He took me on a blind date, she said, buttering the toast. My sister had said that if I went to nursing school, I would drop out and marry a farmer from Lost Creek. She was right.

I thought about water that slips under the mossy stones, runs beneath the skin of the earth.

Was he a farmer then? I said.

He was an oiler on a power shovel, at a strip mine near Smith Chapel. When he came for me, he had a fresh haircut, wore a suit and tie. In the alley behind my boardinghouse, he took out his guitar, serenaded me with Ernest Tubb songs. I hated country music! I slammed the window—but I was too late.

I thought about his hands, cracked in the winter, smeared with pine sap, ash, and drops of oils from his traps. When he was young, he skinned animals, and scraped off the gristle and fat, and nailed pelts of skunk to a series of planks.

Did you and he both think about not showing up for the wedding? I said.

It was raining that day, my grandmother said, laughing. *He had some repairs he wanted to finish. At the time, he was hauling coal, driving a dump truck. It wasn't steady work.*

■ ■ ■

One spring when his children were small, my grandfather did what he had to do: he took his gun to the edge of the field at the woods line, where red-bellied woodpeckers hammered the trees, where animal eyes glowed on the darkest nights. In the lean years, in the early years, he took his gun and shot a fox squirrel with a mouthful of leaves, he shot a fox squirrel carrying a length of grapevine. They had been collecting materials for the loose masses that they nested in. Two limp bodies in rusty coats. When my grandfather saw no more fox squirrels, he took his gun into the deep woods, went looking for the smaller grey squirrels he sometimes saw there, sometimes did not.

From his bloody hands, my grandmother took the headless squirrel bodies. She singed the bodies to burn away any stray hairs. Bodies like puppets, like dolls. She washed them in several waters, wiped them dry with an old dishtowel. She cut them into neat pieces or quartered them, she rubbed salt and pepper over them, rolled them in flour or fine cornmeal, dipped them in egg if she had an egg. She made fried squirrel and gravy, she made squirrel and dumplings. She stewed squirrels in salted water until their bones were pink, until their meat was tender, falling off the bones.

■ ■ ■

At sunset, I walk to the top of my grandparents' knob. I take in the acres they mowed and fenced, the rust-roofed sheds and pale silo. And the diminishing pond in deep shadow, the goldenrod and multiflora rose.

I can begin here.

I try to bring back as much of them as I can. For me, for my sons. I am thinking about the burning planet where they will live.

Once, I walked with my grandfather, stood with him on the knob. He pointed his hand and named for me the adjacent counties. And maybe he also said Texas Mountain, Pifer Mountain, and Laurel, Limestone, Polecat, the long folded ridges, the western edge of the Alleghenies. Maybe he thought about the starving Confederate soldiers on Laurel Mountain, who had surrendered for a wagon of hard bread. The ridges bounded us, as if we were looking out from the middle of a fancy bowl, scalloped and grey-green, the color of pond water.

That was before the windfarm was built on Laurel Mountain, before turbines and batteries in steel boxes were

I try to bring back as much of them as I can. For me, for my sons. I am thinking about the burning planet where they will live.

installed, before their red blinkers flashed warnings every night. Before cow burps were linked to greenhouse gas, glacial melt. Before the first coyotes came and threatened livestock— eating anything they can chew, the DNR says.

Once, my grandfather baled hay, strung barbed wire, dug fence holes, clipped bull calves. I think his work was a strain of love.

Once, a sinkhole opened in the meadow where the red and white-faced cattle grazed. My grandfather told me some settler a hundred years back had mined the farm. I thought about the unseen cavities lacing his fields, an understory of tunnels where someone had dug out the coal.

On my hands and knees, face in a ring of earth, I peered in, and felt, or almost felt, a draft, a cool shivery gust that smelled like ashes and old leaves. I took in an impossible underground room, black and jagged, shiny and unlit.

■ ■ ■

My grandmother rode with me to the department store, bought a new dress shirt for my grandfather. He would have it, along with his grey slacks and bus driving shoes, to wear when he slept in the earth.

At his funeral, standing near him in the long box, my grandmother greeted each mourner, gave each a glance, a word, a nod, then turned her eyes back to him. Once, she said, *He looks good in that shade of blue.* A relative corrected her: *He's not really here,* meaning only the spirit has ceaseless life. She replied, *Yes, but I love what's still here.*

Our family wouldn't listen to his song tapes or look at pictures of him, waiting until danger of missing him too much had passed.

Come spring, she will look for trout lily in the ravine. Will crumble soil with her arthritic fingers. Will make two gardens. Will mix Miracle-Gro granules. Will plant snap peas so that she can freeze them later on, have the taste of springtime when she thaws them in January.

Come fall, she will try to fill a big sinkhole in the back yard. She will move gravel, haul loads of rocks from the garden in her cart, get some extra shale and work at shoveling it in for two hours. When it still isn't filled, she will cover it over with boards.

She will hang shiny pie pans and strips of foil to protect her gardens from crows, and put a radio among the tomatoes and play rock music, heavy metal, screaming guitars, leave it blaring all night to scare away the deer. She will plant corn in the long lines, seed by seed.

■ ■ ■

And then I move to Tennessee, four hundred miles away, and I don't see her as much as I would like.

Years pass by.

I can continue with this: spring again, and new moon peas, peepers crying in the swamp below her house, cabbage plants, onion sets. The season of cracking open, and bloodroot, and egg strings. Without him. My grandmother carries the rocks away, chops the cloddy ground.

The spring peeper, a small chorus frog, lives in the pond she and my grandfather sank in, shearing cattails below the waterline. Maybe they saw *frogs an inch long, blue-ash, with dark stripes,* sunning on sunken logs, *on tussocks, swimming among floating debris.* The season of pour out, swell up, jewelweed and monkey flower.

My grandmother hears the peepers calling, a rattle that rises, recedes, *like a scraping coarse-toothed comb.* Maybe he's gone on ahead but isn't far away, has gone past the boulders and outcrops he calls the big rocks, has gone into the trackless woods. Maybe she's waiting to follow him. How many. She lists, and snags, and thins. All the time she tries to catch a ballad, plaint, what he sings from the next, the after. ■

FRINGES

Patsy Cline courage
breaks the flower pot.

That's where I was
planted. With power

and certitude, I tried and
tried to blossom. It worked.

We didn't know our own
strength until it caused

a decided destruction.
Now, speak my name.

MAURA WAY

SHREDDING MY BROTHER

The Paper Shredder is sensitive & refuses unopened letters, demands surgery
    to extract everything rotting inside unassuming envelopes

but how deceitful! — they are looming with receipts for his punctured lungs
    from hospitals that healed the wrong inside.

E-ZPass scrapes & licks my brother's bones. Speeding tickets bloat
    until they are blue with want. I am annihilating parts of him

that take up too much space, which is everything that remind us
    he was a wound.

Hungry for his name, The Paper Shredder wonders what I will do
    with credit card offers & magazine subscriptions,

which remind us of nothing. I tuck them under ancient photographs
    of his little baby face, pink & stupid.

SARAH GRACE GOOLDEN

SAVANNAH, CONFUSED BY TWO LESBIANS WEARING MASKS

The man in the red shirt across the bar's white noise
is swallowing us in the hungry stare of a carnivore at a farm,

surrounded by the sweet pink meat
of a cow still annoyingly alive.

If nothing else, he is shackled to his shamelessness
as he refuses to blink over his warm beer,

lest he miss the revolution raging
in our hands folded into a deadbolt.

I can only imagine the cannibalistic catastrophe
taking place as he tries to understand

the existence of our fatty flesh
as excluded from the menu

of his quiet wife, lolling her straw around a pink drink
& sipping his silence.

SARAH GRACE GOOLDEN

PURE

(with a line by Gillian Welch)

On my twenty-ninth birthday, a girl named
after an accent presses *god moves on the water like casey jones*

into my left shoulder blade. I dream the ink rubs out
like a stitch, perhaps to signify my erasure, or resurrection.

It's one of the first things you noticed about me. The tattoo.
I don't like explaining it to people, which I think you liked

even more. It's a song, I'll say. The music wasn't enough for us.
Sometimes I forget the words are there. Then, I change.

LAUREN SMOTHERS

JAYNE MOORE WALDROP

I n "For What It's Worth," one of the stories that populate Jayne Moore Waldrop's tender, linked story collection *Drowned Town*, a character muses about "generational labor." The notion is at the heart of this book, which considers how the federal government's seizure of land in western Kentucky to create two lakes (Kentucky Lake and Lake Barkley) and a recreation area (Land Between the Lakes) displaced and impacted a cast of characters across several generations. Each is deeply drawn: the real estate appraiser grappling with the true worth of a family's homeplace, the inmate from the mountains coming to terms with his surroundings and landscape, and the woman—a teacher, wife, and mother—adrift and struggling with depression. But at the heart of the book lies a friendship between two women—Cam and Margaret—who, despite physical separations and the occasional periods of tension that emerge in lifelong relationships, remain tied to each other and to their place of origin. All the while, Waldrop shies away from offering easy, pat answers to the dilemma of whether the government's action was correct or justified. Instead, she dives headlong into the complexities, showing both the sacrifices made by the families and communities displaced by the seizure, as well as the benefits brought to the region, including hydroelectric power, flood control, recreation, and economic advances.

In a telephone conversation, Waldrop discussed *Drowned Town* with *Appalachian Review* editor Jason Kyle Howard, musing upon the collection's themes and her own history and relationship with the lakes, and her ancestral ties to the mountains.

■ ■ ■

JKH: When did the idea for *Drowned Town* begin to take shape for you?

JMW: It began to take shape when I noticed that so much of what I was writing was based around the lakes [Kentucky Lake and Lake Barkley in west Kentucky] and Land Between the Lakes. I was fairly well into it—I had written several stories—and I kept coming back to this theme of loss in this place. It continued to grow in my mind that this history has

Jayne Moore Waldrop

never been written from a more personal perspective. There are some excellent nonfiction books about the building of the lakes, the building of the dams, and the taking of Land Between the Lakes, but it had never been written about from a more personal viewpoint, and that's what I wanted to show. And it just seemed like these stories—as I wrote—every time I tried to write a new story, it was always about the lakes, so eventually I caught on that they were linked and they were telling the same story but from different people's perspectives, different characters.

JKH: Why do you think that the lakes have been such a source of imagination and inspiration for you?

JMW: I guess because I grew up being on the lakes a lot. From childhood we would go to the public beach at Kentucky Dam Village State Park, so we were always connected to the lake, and then as a teenager I often had friends who had either a place on the lake—their families did—or a boat for skiing. My sister and I, particularly, spent a lot of time in LBL hiking, so I think I am just naturally drawn to water. I love being on the water, seeing the water. I think that's a function of growing up in Paducah, where rivers are a major part of the landscape and also of life. Western Kentucky just has so many large, significant rivers that it's hard not to be connected to water growing up there. So, I always thought of it as a source of recreation, a source of beauty, but since I didn't have a personal connection to those places that were lost from the construction, I never really considered the sacrifices, and it was only well into adulthood that I started thinking about the scale of the environmental changes in western Kentucky. I'm not sure there is another area in Kentucky that has been as affected in such a concentrated dose with these enormous dams that are just two miles apart, and then the taking of the land to become a national recreation area. The scale of the changes is enormous, and not a lot of people know that about western Kentucky.

JKH: No, I don't think they do either. One of the many things I love about this collection is that it's populated with ordinary people living out their lives—trying to get by, making good and bad choices, working and living against the backdrop of this place. It honors people whose lives are so often overlooked or forgotten or neglected. In thinking about the collection, I'm wondering why do you believe the stories of everyday people are worth telling?

JMW: Because I grew up in a family that's what you'd call "everyday people." That's my experience of life and the people I'm from. One of the reasons I love fiction so much is that it allows the reader to step into the shoes of a character—whether that is an everyday person or a "fancy" person—to learn what that character is going through and to feel what they're going through, and I think that's related to understanding what many people's lives are about. It's the small beauties and the small tragedies in everyday life that I'm really interested in because, as most of us know, living in the present is all about noticing these small beauties and small flaws, small tragedies in life.

JKH: I love that—"the small beauties and small tragedies"—and these characters experience those. There are so many different characters present in these stories, and I'm wondering which ones do you feel closest to? This might be like trying to choose between favorites, which is always a hard question, at least for me. But I'm wondering

which of these characters you feel closest to? Which were the most rewarding, or which were the hardest, to write?

JMW: I feel close to several of the characters for different reasons, and that's one of the reasons I wanted to write about so many people who are connected to this place to not tell just one individual story or one family story or even one community story. The scale is so broad. I feel close to the two women characters—Cam and Margaret—because I think they represent long-term friendship. They represent women at middle age. They're well into their forties by the time the current action is occurring in the story, and they've been through a lot together. They've had losses. They've had sadness. They've had great joy together in their friendship, and they've really grown through that relationship. I think they are opposites in many ways, but they contribute to each other's lives in a yin-and-yang perspective. They don't have to be exactly alike, but they grow through their relationship, and I think that's true with any long-term friendship. A friendship that lasts will have an ebb and flow to it, but there's an enrichment that comes from having a close friend to rely on. I think that I want to represent them—by the time they reach middle age—as still having a lot of life and a lot of decisions and a lot of choices about everything that is to come…I guess that's writing what I know—that there are lots of important and good choices that can come with middle age and with aging…In that way I feel close to those two characters.

I also feel close to the other characters who are experiencing different kinds of loss—it's all in the context of loss of place with the changes that have occurred in western Kentucky—but there are so many other forms of loss in the stories from loss of freedom through the prisoner in the Kentucky State

Penitentiary. He, to me, is a really compelling character because his life sentence was not of his making. Someone else made that decision for him. He was an accessory to a heinous crime, but his imprisonment was pursuant to the law but not of his own making. I feel like he represents so many others in western Kentucky. Their homes, their communities, their places were taken in the name of the public interest, pursuant to the law, but there was no real effective way of fighting that or challenging it, so I just think of him being in this place, and it was very foreign to him. He is a character who came from eastern Kentucky. Actually, this crime that occurred took place where my dad's family is from, so I'm connected to that place in the story. And he comes to this place that is so unfamiliar and unlike anything he's used to—being imprisoned and transferred to the state penitentiary at the other end of the state.

JKH: And Kentucky's a long state!

JMW: It's a very long state, and he's never seen a place like this. That's one thing that's true about Kentucky is the landscape changes east to west significantly. Also, there's one character, Elmer, who is a land appraiser, and I feel particularly close to Elmer and also to Nate McCracken who is losing his family farm between the rivers—a farm that had been held for generations, a farm that had sustained his family since shortly after the Civil War—so the connection of those two characters is really important. The appraiser comes to see the value of place in a way he's not seen before. It's always been this very objective viewpoint of value always based on the numbers.

JKH: I'm obsessed both as a writer and as a reader with structure, and I'm always intrigued by linked story

collections. In *Drowned Town* those connections are sometimes obvious. Sometimes they're more subtle. Could you talk about those points of connection and how and why you chose to structure the book that way? Did those links appear on the page organically, or did you craft them consciously?

JMW: Those links occurred organically because I didn't really set out to make these connections. They just continued to bubble up, but the linking of these stories is sort of organic [and is] based on the Cumberland River in many ways, because the stories seemed to meander across Kentucky like the Cumberland River does from [eastern Kentucky] through Nashville, where some of the stories are set, and then on up into western Kentucky as the river turns and heads north to the Ohio. So, there were a few points in making those connections that they had to be a little more intentional, but I didn't really set out to write linked stories. I set out to write what I thought was going to be a novel, and I'm guessing it turned out to be a novel-in-stories in a way. I'm not sure the difference of linked stories or a novel in stories. It's kind of a fine point, but the structure is kind of a different structure because I wanted to travel not only back and forth in time but also with all these different characters and all these different settings, so there is a meandering and a wandering with it. The reason I did that—this was very intentional—is I didn't want to only talk about or have characters that existed at the time of the damming of the Cumberland or the taking of Land Between the Lakes. It was very important for me to show this ebb and flow of time so that the changes that occurred in western Kentucky didn't end as soon as the lake rose. This is a multi-generational impact of loss of home, so I wanted to show what happened at the time with the people experiencing those changes at the time, but I also wanted to show the lingering impact.

JKH: And the reverberations. [That craft choice is] one of my favorite parts of the book, and I think it adds so many other layers. I'm a believer that the writing of books, when you sit down to write a book, that the book itself teaches you a lesson or a series of lessons. What do you think *Drowned Town* **taught you?**

JMW: To look beneath the surface of any character, and I'm going to give you an example of Margaret [a hard-driven Louisville attorney]. When I first wrote her, she was a very disagreeable, unlikeable character, and it was only through working with her and as the stories were revised that we looked beyond her initial unlikeable-ness. She had her own backstory, and I think that's what I like to show in any of the characters, that humans are multilayered. I think so often we think of particularly rural characters—there is a real strong rural-urban balance in this book and a tension as well as balance [and] I don't want to have a one-dimensional, rural stereotype. The people I'm writing about, the people who inspired this, deserve more than a stereotypical portrayal. I'd like for people to see with this book that life and place can be very different than first impressions. When you visit western Kentucky and these places, you see this beautiful landscape and these amazing lakes, but there is a history there that is so much deeper than what you see.

JKH: You're a lawyer by training, and you practiced for many years before leaving the profession to focus on other areas of your life. As someone who nearly went to law school, I'm curious about how those years of training

and practice might interact with your life now as a writer. How do you think that those two professions—these two iterations of your life—interact?

JMW: I don't think they're as far apart as you might think, because I think the ability to write is critical in the legal practice. The ability to communicate ideas and advocate are also critical in the legal practice, so I don't think it's as a big a leap as it might seem. I think my legal training and my desire to get the facts correct on the historical side of this fiction is really important. The ability to research the history that provides the historical setting is very important, and that's a skill that is learned in law school and in legal practice, and I think just the knowledge of the powers of eminent domain is also an important part of my research for this book.

JKH: And you used the legal phrase earlier, "pursuant to the law." I was thinking as you were saying that—

JMW: It sounds very lawyerly, doesn't it!

JKH: It does, but [I'm also thinking about] having that language and that deep reservoir of knowledge with this book that is so centered on—at least a narrative thread— the law and how the law can interact with place and people and cause conflict.

JMW: It's an important part of the story that has to be recognized—that [this] is the way our system is set up, that there are to be projects in the public interest, and the government has that power. While it has created many opportunities in western Kentucky—these federal projects for flood control and hydroelectric power and navigation—

all those are important public interests. I wanted to remain somewhat neutral on that, [not] saying "those decisions were wrong or bad." My goal was to show that they occurred, and I also wanted to acknowledge the price that some people paid, and those were a lot of farmers and people who lived in small towns who bore the brunt of these decisions. I didn't want to take sides, but I want to acknowledge both sides, that there are legitimate interests on both sides.

JKH: And leave it up to the reader to piece some of that together.

JMW: And for the reader to be aware that these types of projects and this type of progress doesn't come without impact to the local community.

JKH: It's been a big year for you. In May, your poetry chapbook *Pandemic Lent: A Season in Poems* was released by Finishing Line Press. What was the inspiration for those poems?

JMW: That book came up in an interesting and unexpected way because I had just reader Brother Paul Quenon's book, *In Praise of the Useless Life*—his memoir. He is a monk at the Abbey of Gethsemani in Nelson County, and I just read his book and loved it. He talked about writing haiku as a way of focusing on the moment, particularly in a spiritual sense. So, in February of 2020, I decided for Lent 2020 I would write a haiku a day as part of a Lenten practice rather than giving up alcohol or chocolate for Lent, I decided I would write a haiku to capture that moment.

JKH: And then the whole world went to hell!

JMW: It sure did! And about a week after the project was when we had our first case of Covid-19 in Kentucky, and things shut down, and life changed. It became a completely different project. Like many writers during those early stages of the pandemic, it was hard to focus on writing. It was hard to concentrate and come up with anything creative. It was such a heavy, dark time. So, what I had expected to be a fairly easy project of doing three lines a day, of five-seven-five syllables became the only writing that I was doing at the time because it was a distressing time. By the time I got to the end of Lent, I had lots and lots of haikus. Some days I wrote a lot more than others, and it turned into a book.

JKH: Although you were raised in west Kentucky, your family has deep roots in the mountains in eastern Kentucky. How do you think that ancestry has informed your writing?

JMW: My ancestry is important to so much of what I do. My family had such a large impact on the way I see the world. I also know what the impact of dislocation is and outmigration because my parents left eastern Kentucky during a particularly significant downturn in that coal economy. They left in the early 1950s, so I was the only one of their children who was born in western Kentucky, so I had a different perspective. Growing up, I straddled being a western Kentuckian with this strong Appalachian influence from my parents, whether that was in the way they grew a garden, the way they had to have a little land around them, or the words they used, their choices of words. It's very different than most of the people I grew up with, so I felt like I had a strong Appalachian influence in my life even though I never lived there. I think it informs my writing because—like in *Drowned Town*—dislocation and that yearning for home is a really important theme, and I saw that in my parents for as long as they were living. Home was always the mountains, although they lived in Paducah the rest of their lives after they moved. So sixty-plus years of living in Paducah, but you go up home to the mountains. That yearning for home and the memory of home is something that really influences all of my writing.

JKH: The lakes have been drawing you back, and I know you have plans to eventually move to be on one of the them. How do you envision the perfect day spent there?

JMW: A perfect day would be both in the woods in Land Between the Lakes on one of the magnificent hiking trails, and then the afternoon and evening until sunset spent out on the water. That would be an ideal day for me because it's capturing both the woods and the lake, and the lake, for me, is really important because it connects all the things that I love. That would be my ideal day. One of the things I love about both places is that they are for the general public. There is no requirement that you have to pay admission or that you have to have a fancy boat to be out on the lake. They are available to everyone, and that makes it even more important to me. There are no memberships you have to have this recreation in your life, so I appreciate the fact that these areas provide recreation for that "every person."

JKH: They're egalitarian.

JMW: That's important to me. There are some fancy boats, but you don't have to have that. There are some excellent public beaches all up and down the lake. It's available. It's not exclusionary. ◼

TO MARY OLIVER

I learned to press night owls,
grasshoppers and wild geese between
pages like dried lily petals, keepsakes for later,
like the way I savor every letter of your poems—
like they could tell me something
I don't already know. Except,
      I already own the connection between
the green of the mother and the red
of my tongue, can taste the heron's
cry, and know to never shy from the dirt.
Even on carpet, stories above the ground, I feel
      the snap of the snare stringing me
upside down, and the impression I swing
into the world. Though I never venture
into the woods, I know that ivy is slick, that moss
can be crunchy, that even dead trees can live
forever, that rings rot but roots dig, that water
can be hard and soft and jagged and lacey and slimy and
      will eat everything. Though I've never
heard a bloated tic's heart-beat or smelled the side
of a deer, I have lived in a hundred different
bodies, am tethered to the one-day fly, the fuzzy
bottomed bee, and the lonely long-beaked
stork. I don't have to spend a lifetime perched
above water or walking in woods to know
I belong with the hummingbirds, carried away
by a violent gale, and with the voles,
      digging with little hands into the earth.

MEGAN GOWER

KNEE DEEP

We went for a hike the day after a blizzard, the day after our fight, drove right over icy roads of the Blue Ridge Parkway, where a single drift of the tires, adrift from single lane highway would have slipped us into the rock. It was another universe—devoid of color, only white sky, white grass, white solid lake, every path unmarked, every pocket of earth frozen in newness, cemented in the softness of erasure. Go where you want, the snow whispered, offering no options, no roads, and we had nowhere else to go but back, but we could never go back, so we tip-toed forward along the ridge, hoping not to slope into a ravine, not to be seen by the honest sun, or eaten by a hungry wolf. The gulf which had stretched white and endless like the landscape hurdled in smaller, seeped through the layers of our clothing, through our coats, and we stayed quiet so as not to disturb the quivering, quaking calm, and sunk our knees deep into something

more.

MEGAN GOWER

GRACKLE

Black bird opens its beak,
　　　　voice creaking like the tuning
　　　　　　　　of an old car radio
　　　　　　　　　　　　searching for frequencies.

Three of them
　　　　in the tree out back
　　　　　　　　speak in crackling
　　　　　　　　　　　　waves and vibrations—calling.

I try to tune in, want to listen
　　　　to the hits, watch how they groove
　　　　　　　　along the branch with spotty connection and beat
　　　　　　　　　　　　each other with their wings.

I wonder what they sing,
　　　　what warning they're emitting—
　　　　　　　　to look out, to fly home—
　　　　　　　　　　　　to fly from what plagues us.

They close their throats,
　　　　bob their heads,
　　　　　　　　their shrill eyes still
　　　　　　　　　　　　pierce the veil of rain.

MEGAN GOWER

WHERE I WAS

Ask me again one day
why panthers never drink
from still water.

I know this slender hour well
and I've learned not to ask
much from it, and that

what keeps you up
will not soon go away.
But I'll tell you this: Once

an imperfect noun
fell from a persimmon tree
half a couplet before noon.

It rolled down a slope
that never thought to be a verb,
and it pressed a long path

through the clover-patch
and to the pond. That's where I was,
carving the cup of splendor

as kingfishers dropped
from the trees like pleasing rain.
And my silence was enough.

JOHN SAAD

TO RAY

INTERVIEWER: *Are you religious?*

*RAYMOND CARVER: No, but I have to believe in
miracles and the possibility of resurrection. No question
about that. Every day that I wake up, I'm glad to wake up.
That's why I like to wake up early. In my drinking days I
would sleep until noon or whatever and I would usually
wake up with the shakes.*
          —The Paris Review *(1983)*

I get it, Ray. I really do. You were
playing it cool when you told *The Paris Review*
"art doesn't make anything happen." But I got something
like the shakes the first time I taught "Cathedral." The class
had just really gotten into it, you know?
And I nearly wept the first time I heard "Late Fragment."
A Baptist preacher read it on Pentecost.
Even so, you'd have enjoyed that sermon, Ray.
That preacher wrapped things up by lighting a corn chip
on fire and raising it like a candle. A corn chip!
Who knew a Frito could light the entire world?
You know, I've wandered your part of the world, Ray.
I've seen those sawmills trucking in Douglas firs,
and I've fished those rivers for steelhead and salmon.
Your Northwest's not so different from my Gulf Coast.
Our native corners share a common language
of rainy timber towns and steely fish,
and of never being all that certain where our bruises
came from once we're awake. But your stories are all over
since, as you say, you've bounced around:
Yakima, Eureka, Iowa City, Palo Alto, Syracuse, Etcetera. I can't say

the same for myself, now almost forty years
in the state I was born in; and still sometimes I feel
so far away from myself, you know? Like I've nearly
forgotten one life already. What do you do
with a feeling like that? I guess you just sit and write
the plainest, most son-of-a-bitch poems you can,
about big debts and bigger fish, junk food
for dinner, and waking early still heavy with sleep.
Poems like "In a Greek Orthodox Church Near Daphne."
Shit, Ray. So many churches so close to home
and one day you and Tess end up near Daphne, Alabama,
at Malbis, the very church I was baptized in in 1982.
Later you found the words for how you favored
the warm evening wind to the brooding Christ of the icons.
It's a good poem, Ray. Maybe not "Gravy" good
or "The Current" good, but good in its honest joy
of man's original pain-in-the-ass-ness. I confess
I'm biased, knowing so well the way those blue
Byzantine towers so weirdly rise out of miles
of tract homes and longleaf pines, and how the wind
smudges each brick with the Gulf of Mexico's brine.
So you can imagine my gladness when
I first read it in *A New Path to the Waterfall.*
After I closed the book, there was your portrait
taking up all that backcover real estate,
your eyebrows brooding like dark sand dunes,
like two heavy salmon leaping towards creation.
And knowing this was your last book, I thought,
Who is the Christ now? Who else can show
us fishermen huddled over an oil drum fire?
Or the miracle of finding leftovers at midnight?
Or that each new day on earth is gravy?

I don't care if you weren't religious, Ray. Really,
I don't. Sometimes I'm not either, and that's okay.
But don't say art doesn't make anything happen,
even when you're playing it cool. It does make
things happen. It made you step outside that church
when you needed to meet the wind, Ray. Besides,
that last book sure made Hayden Carruth cry
all over a big piece of goddamn pie
at one-thirty in the morning. And Hayden wrote
about that night at his kitchen table, eating his big pie
of tears, because your words made it happen. Sometimes
a thing only happens because someone loved
it enough to make it into art. That's the world
I want to live in, Ray, and that was your gift.

Well, it's gotten late on me tonight, Ray.
Real late. Like Hayden-late. I've already dug
through the refrigerator twice (no pie)
and watched some godawful western on TV;
and even though I never can recall
what first rouses me from bed each night,
I've thought a lot about your words tonight,
Ray. But now all that's left to wonder is
when morning finally comes, and it'll come
soon, will I go down to the river and see
your heavy scarred fish still holding in the current?

JOHN SAAD

WE'RE VERY SORRY FOR YOUR LOSS

DANA SHAVIN

When Jemma got up, Berger was sitting in the red wingback chair by the open window with a stack of legal briefs in his lap.

"Where's Lila?" said Jemma.

"Out back."

"Did you clean up?"

"I put the sheets in the washer. I think the blood will come out.

Jemma shook her head. "I can't believe I slept this late."

Berger gathered up his papers and set them in the floor, then patted his thighs. Jemma sat down on his lap and leaned into him. A shelf of cool air pushed in through the window, along with the earthy scent of pine mulch. "You were upset," said Berger.

"I'm still upset."

"I know. But Jem, you know, dogs will be dogs."

Jemma didn't say anything.

"Hey, look at me," Berger said. Jemma turned toward him. Wisps of blonde hair, escapees from her short ponytail, framed her face. Berger brushed them back. "It was just a rooster. It's not like she tore apart a kid or anything."

"I know, Berger. But it's sad. And what am I supposed to tell the neighbor? *Oh hi, by the way, my dog ate your pet rooster, sorry about that.*" She stood up.

"Where are you going?"

"To clean up the front yard before she sees the evidence."

"I'll do it," said Berger. "I just needed some coffee first."

Jemma waved him off. "Just make me some coffee," she said.

■ ■ ■

Outside the dew was still heavy on the grass. A smattering of white and brown feathers littered the walkway, like someone had ripped open a down pillow and shaken out the contents. Long threads of gut and muscle, spaghetti-like, glistened in the early sun. A wave of nausea rolled over Jemma as she peeled open a garbage bag, gathered up the feathers, and dropped them in. Then she picked up a stick and speared the bloody innards. No sooner had she dropped what was left of the rooster into the bag than she heard her neighbor across the way calling him.

"Cockadoodle-doo!" The neighbor waited several seconds, then called again: "Cockadoodle-doo!" Jemma could see her turning round and round, scanning the perimeter of her yard for the rooster, who came running every morning on his spindly little legs, squawking loudly in anticipation of cracked corn.

"Cockadoodle doo! Breakfast!" the neighbor called, still turning in her yard, one hand over her eyes, shielding them from the sun. When she caught sight of Jemma she dropped her hand and headed over. Jemma's heart started to pound. What would she say, really, when the neighbor asked whether she'd seen her rooster. *Cockadoodle-doo got into my yard last night*, seemed a good beginning. Not only was it was true, more importantly, it put the onus for what came next on the rooster rather than on Lila. She threw the stick and the garbage bag into the bushes and walked up to the road.

The neighbor wasn't that old, maybe sixty-five, but she walked with a pronounced limp, like one leg was shorter than the other. Her pants were baggy and she wore an oversized man's T-shirt which, Jemma could see when she got closer, appeared not to have been washed in some time. Jemma felt sorry for her. As she waited at the mailbox for the neighbor to get to her, she thought what a bad idea it was to name an animal the sound it made. Lila's name wouldn't be Lila but something ridiculous and embarrassing to call out, like *Broof*.

"Good morning," said Jemma when the neighbor finally got to her. The neighbor grabbed the mailbox for support. She was breathing hard. "You seen my rooster?" she asked.

"Um, not lately," Jemma said, which was sort of the truth, if you didn't count seeing the rooster's insides as seeing the rooster.

"Lord I hope nothin's done got' im." The neighbor turned back and scanned her own yard again from the vantage point of Jemma's mailbox. Her husband had died a few months earlier, of a heart attack, right in their driveway. Jemma was getting ready for work when she heard the neighbor scream. She ran to the window and saw the husband flat on his back on the ground, his wife crouched beside him, screaming and smacking at his chest and arms. Jemma ran over to help but it was already too late. A coffee can lay on its side next to the husband, corn fanning out in a wide arc like spilled marbles, while Cockadoodle-doo, frightened by the commotion, ran in circles beside them, flapping his wings and squawking loudly. Jemma decided it wouldn't hurt to let the woman hold out hope that Cockadoodle was just out wandering the neighborhood and would come home soon.

"I just know one day he's gonna get in the road and get hisself hit," said the neighbor. People drive too fast through here, I don't know what's their hurry." She gave her head a fierce right-left shake and spit something hard and whitish into the grass. "Who's that?"

Jemma turned toward the house just as the door slammed. Berger was making his way to the end of the driveway. "My boyfriend Berger," she said.

Berger extended his hand to the neighbor a full four steps before reaching the end of the driveway. The neighbor looked at it, then took it with three fingers and wiggled it.

"I done lost Cockadoodle-doo," she said.

"Berger's a lawyer," Jemma said. "Right, Berger?" She gave him an exaggerated, wide-eyed look, wordlessly imploring him not to say anything about the previous night's events.

"Well I sure would like to sue whoever's done got my rooster," the neighbor said.

"He's a car-accident lawyer." Jemma knew Berger hated when she called him that, but she only did it to shorthand conversation with people who might not otherwise understand what it was he did.

"*Personal In*jury," Berger always said, biting down on his words. "There is more to the world of *injury* than *vehicles*."

"That rooster's all I got," said the neighbor.

Jemma told her they'd keep an eye out for Cockadoodle-doo. When they got back in the house, Berger sat down at the kitchen table with his papers and Jemma pulled bread and eggs out of the refrigerator. A wave of exhaustion washed over her, and she put the eggs back. She didn't know how long she'd slept before the rooster attack. She remembered hearing the rustle of brush beneath her window and Lila's low, guttural growl. She'd hovered on the continuum between sleep and wakefulness, her mind indecisive about a call to action, when the bushes exploded with Lila's vicious surprise attack and the *screech-screech* of the terrified bird. By the time Jemma

Jemma screamed at her, pushed her off the crumpled, quivering bird and crouched over him, her heart pounding in her ears.

got outside, Lila had the rooster pinned, and was ripping him open like a present. Jemma screamed at her, pushed her off the crumpled, quivering bird and crouched over him, her heart pounding in her ears. Steam from the open body cavity warmed her face as blood seeped into the grass. The next thing she knew, Berger was pulling her up off the cold, wet grass, saying, "Come on Jemma, come on, it's over," and she let him lead her back into the house, following the trail of bloody paw prints through the kitchen and down the hallway, past the spare bedroom where Lila, satisfied she'd done her job, was already curled, loop-de-loops of blood on the cream flannel sheets where she had turned three times before lying down. The whole attack lasted all of five, maybe ten seconds.

Jemma poured a mug of coffee and dropped the bread in the toaster. She turned around and leaned against the counter. "I have to tell her at some point," she said.

"No you don't."

"It seems cruel to just let her wonder."

"Sometimes a lie is kinder than the truth."

"This from a lawyer," said Jemma.

"You know what I mean."

"If I don't tell her the truth, she can't grieve properly."

"People grieve loss, not detail," said Berger.

Jemma sipped her coffee. The last thing she remembered before being pulled away from the rooster was hovering over his warm insides, sickened at the sight of the gelatinous, quivering organs. She had only seen two other dead things up close: the dog she'd put to sleep two years earlier, and her father. She'd held the dog in her arms as it died, so the transition had been gradual, but her father had already been dead a full two hours by the time she made it to the hospital. She knew it would haunt her if she didn't get all the facts so she made her mother recount the timeline of events as she'd gotten them from the hospital staff: how her father had gotten up in the night without calling a nurse, hemorrhaged in the bathroom, then fallen and hit his head on the toilet. At some point in the timeline (no one, not even the doctor knew when exactly), errant blood cells crowded the narrow hallways of his heart like Friday afternoon commuters rushing for the first train out of the city, causing a blockage. As her mother told her the details, the doctor pushed into the room.

"This is my daughter," Jemma's mother said.

"Your father was out of bed against doctor's orders," the doctor said, looking at Jemma sternly, as if she were somehow responsible. Jemma's mother glared at him for several seconds and then, without warning, grabbed her key ring from the bedside table and hurled it at him. It glanced him in the forehead and opened a small cut just below the hairline. The doctor put his fingers to it, stunned, and then, as if Jemma's mother had literally knocked sense into him, said, "We're very sorry for your loss," and left the room.

"People grieve both," Jemma said.

"What?" Berger said.

"People need resolution. Their grief needs a destination. It's why they pull drowning victims from lakes and mail home the bodies of soldiers."

Berger nodded. "Tell her then," he said.

Lila was in the back yard, curled under the rose bush. Jemma got her leash from the hook by the door and fastened it to her collar. Of course people needed resolution. Cockadoodle-doo might not have done much beyond showing up for breakfast on time, but who was Jemma to sentence the one person—to whom that meant so much—to a lifetime of uncertainty? Of all people, Berger should have understood this. He was right, there was a world of injury beyond vehicles. Other people, if they weren't careful, were that world.

As Jemma and Lila made their way up the neighbor's driveway, Jemma could see a tiny light on in the kitchen window. Her heart was heavy in her chest as she knocked on the door.

The neighbor looked surprised to see her again so soon. The morning newspaper sat on the kitchen table, unopened, next to the coffee can full of cracked corn.

"Cockadoodle-doo—" Jemma had rehearsed what she was going to say, but suddenly she couldn't remember the line, the one that said the rooster made his own bed.

"You seen him out there?" asked the neighbor, her face brightening, reaching for the can of corn.

"No." Jemma closed her eyes. "Yes. Actually, I saw a car hit him." She had no idea where the words came from. "Last night, late. It was going really fast, there's no way Cockadoodle-doo could have felt a thing. I doubt the driver even saw him." If she was going to stage the ending of least pain for Cockadoodle-doo and the neighbor, she might as well take precautions with the fictitious driver's feelings as well. "I'm sorry I didn't tell you sooner. I knew how upsetting it would be."

The neighbor's eyes, which had widened, brimmed with tears. She held her hand to her mouth for several seconds. "Poor Cockadoodle-doo," she said, shaking her head. "Well I can't say I'm surprised." Then she looked at the floor and smoothed her T-shirt. "I know people think I'm crazy 'cause I got a rooster for a best friend."

"I don't think you're crazy," Jemma said. "I've got a lawyer for a best friend."

To her surprise, the neighbor looked up at her and laughed a shallow, smoky laugh. She wiped her eyes with the hem of her shirt, then bent down and cupped Lila's chin. "I bet you're a very good dog, aren't you?" she said softly.

Lila sat. ■

GALWAY TRIPTYCH

I.
Language being
a precarious thing,
the phrase tilts

forward how
prepositions set
you on some

specific road
comfortable
until the deer flash

of a foreign word
becomes a man's
tongue in your

mouth more
animal the kiss
a dropped bird

II.
Language being
treason between
your teeth

the way a river
speaks bites
better at it

the wolf
face of the Corrib
and its muscle

undercurrent to
chokehold men
pulled like

heavy seeds
to its stone
floor

III.
Language still
being even after
the vocal chords

shutter off
the chatter through
the arterial street

a fat drop
of quiet folding
midnights to

a single
bronze barglow,
a quivering string

pauses blood
how a guitar
can replace a throat

KELLY ZANOTTI

WATER HORSE

Convinced now
you were only
a water horse

formed from the
cobalt flesh
of the Corrib

your horse
throat
swallowing

the spell I let
you run your
velvet ears

inside me like
this tale a
glass box

like the glass
water you
didn't shatter

when you
rose
sunset

the way the
Corrib stays
not evil but

other

fathering
leather beings
like you

constricting
the bright
seed still

waiting
in the dip
of my breast

and this is
how we
fools die

KELLY ZANOTTI

AFTER ST KEVIN AND THE BLACKBIRD

And since the whole thing's imagined anyhow
—Seamus Heaney

Imagine St Kevin leaning far over heaven's balustrade, aspergillum in hand, surveying Glendalough. Imagine the saint then sprinkling the surface of the Upper Lake to rise and flood his earthly bed cut into the battered rockface below the Spinc ridge. On to the rest of the isle, he rises above county after county, sprinkling the circled stones of Cork, the cillíní of Galway mistakable for outcrops, dousing the peace lines in Belfast with their tribal graffiti—Catholic nationalist and Protestant unionist alike—as the water, no less holy for puddling wallside in the stoups of potholes, greys more, greys more like sullage at first and then pales with time and clears. Keep imagining and next thing you are the pilgrim guided by a blackbird on the wing. Cresting Wicklow Gap, you see the bird, which crested well before you, rise slowly back into view perched like a finial on the selfsame-colored wooden post there that waymarks St Kevin's Way; it flies off at your approach. It leads you downslope and along the Glendasan river to where the ground gives undersole, where mud catches at your steps so that you must arch them more and more against discalceation. Then, dragging up one heel followed by the other from stuckedness, your sandals get sucked off your feet, leaving tracks that sprout toes the moment you walk into Glendalough.

ZACHARY BARTLES

STELLA, IN THE UPSTAIRS ROOM

KAREN SALYER McELMURRAY

A story passed down to me from my mother's people was about a woman named Stella. During the 1930s, Stella, it was said, lived in an upstairs room at a brother's and never left the house. The historical facts are vague. She was a distant cousin of mine, or a great-aunt, and her sequestered life was in Dwale, Kentucky. I imagine her with long, copper-colored hair, a braid winding down her back. She loved the garden below her window, its sunflowers and ripe tomatoes. I think of her alone in her room with bisque-faced dolls for whom she crocheted dresses, and the fine handiwork she might have done—pillowcases with initials and roses. I do know that she never married, a thing summed up both acceptably and unacceptably in the phrase *maiden lady*. What I heard most often about Stella concerned her strangeness. *Odd-turned. Not right in the head.* The Stella-stories were tinged with secrecy, and though I searched family history books I was never able to find out very much about her.

At one point, I wrote a short story about Stella. The entirety of the story takes place on one day, when she is completely alone in the house. The action is her making her way downstairs and out to the front porch, where she sits listening to the chilly fall wind from the mountains. She sings a song I made up and put in her mouth. *The wind blows down, the wind blows back, the wind blows cold and that's a fact.* In a later version of the story, I gave Stella a small bell which she threaded onto a piece of twine and hung from the porch rafters, so she could hear it even when she went back to her upstairs room.

The real Stella passed through the rips and tears in collective memory. I'm not sure if she was a Gray or a Calhoun, and I think, but I am not sure, that she was my grandfather's aunt. I have no one to ask about her history, especially now that most of my ancestors are gone. This much I know must have been true. Glass, back then, wasn't exactly clear. Panes had odd waves and imperfections. Looking into an upstairs window from the yard, you must have seen only an impression, almost a ghost of a woman. Looking out through that beveled glass, Stella would have seen a subdued world, a hushed brilliance that passed as light.

■ ■ ■

As a writer of memoir and personal essays, I've often confronted the question of what should or should not be told when it comes to writing truth. When writing a memoir about surrendering a child to adoption, more than one family member suggested that the story would better written as a novel. I've many times heard criticism of my propensity to tell raw stories, ones that explore what happened, when, and why. During a recent trip back to Kentucky, a dear friend encouraged me to write a novel about my time in Greece many years ago. *Your kin must feel threatened*, she said. *You've told so many of their secrets. Why not write fiction instead?*

I have written secrets, many of them belonging to my family of origin and to my ancestors. I've written about the truths that have been swept into corners, under rugs. The ends of marriages. Infidelity and reckless desire. I've explored pain, both my own and those that must have been inside the hearts of my kin. I've spoken my own history; I've given voice to other unspoken histories that have included mental illnesses. Schizophrenia, obsessive compulsive disorder, bipolar disorder.

Are these stories a betrayal? Are they exploitation? I acknowledge that I've written hard truths, but my hope has been that the telling will provide answers. What does it mean, I've asked my pages again and again, to come from the center of a labyrinth and find one's way out?

■ ■ ■

Secrets fed me when I was small. Night scratching against the window screens. A light filtering beneath a door all night long. Those secrets had explanations I could oftentimes discover the next morning, but I was hungry for more. I write certain events of my childhood over and over, as if the repetition is a spell that just might work if I figured out how. At twelve, I wanted to know what to call the fear I saw in my aunt's eyes—that time they held a cup of coffee to her lips, then walked her back and forth across the kitchen floor. I wanted to know why my grandfather came to live with us for six weeks and what it meant when I overheard my mother whispering to my father. *Psych Ward. Lithium. No choice.* By the time I was thirty, one of my cousins died after struggling with overwhelming depression. No one talked about exactly how Greg died, but for months I dreamed of guns and ropes and deep water. Hunger grew inside me, an emptiness that pressed its little hands inside my chest. Even now, I want to know if it was real, the hunger I remember in the houses of my ancestors: an enormous, mangy bird with hard eyes that wanted and wanted.

■ ■ ■

When I was little, I read every book I could find about secrets, my first favorites being girl mysteries. Nancy Drew. Trixie Belden. A series of Judy Bolton books involved a woman detective, a news reporter named Horace, and a cat named Blackberry. I soon graduated to more complex mysteries—Agatha Christie, Sir Arthur Conan Doyle, Dashiell Hammett. Those, too, soon grew unsatisfactory as I began to long for more intricate secrets. Wilkie Collins still enchants me. *Look where we will,* he wrote. *The inevitable law of revelation is one of the laws of nature: the lasting preservation of a secret is a miracle which the world has never yet seen.* After school, I waited long hours in the garage for my mother to unlock the door and let me come inside. On the sly, I opened boxes of old letters and photographs I found on the shelves beside my father's hand tools. I read between the lines. *I love you, Pearlie,* he wrote to my mother long ago. *I love you like no other woman.*

The mysteries I wanted to solve became more intimate, more complex. At ten and eleven, I went with my father to his office on Sunday afternoons, where we both went to escape my mother, and I read books by the stack from a Department of Education Library on the floor above his. Libraries became my sustenance. By the time I was ten, Margaret Laurence and Sarah Orne Jewett were favorite authors. By twelve, I read with abandon and often with disregard for understanding what I read or why. Edith Wharton. Thomas Hardy. D.H. Lawrence. I read hungrily, devouring the intricacies of relationships, of grief and surrender. I wanted to learn how to solve the secrets right in front of me. I'd come upon my father sitting at his office desk, his head in his hands. What did the unfocused, angry light in my mother's green eyes mean when we came home a half-hour late? Their voices on the other side of my own bedroom wall were a language I couldn't decipher. I studied words and lines, page after page, but found no answers to these secrets.

■ ■ ■

Did Stella have a life before her seclusion in the upstairs room at her brother's house? Her days must have been similar, one to the next. Her room's spare light as she sponged-bathed the familiar lines of her own body. Perhaps she went to church on the occasional Sunday morning. Or perhaps that was too daunting an outing—voices rising in praise, hands clapping so fast sparks rose in the air. Maybe she had to work for days to come up with the courage to spend time alone in the kitchen, but surely, I imagine, she kept a delectable secret there—her love affair with the senses. The dough, sleek and oiled as she turned it out on a floured board. Her hands kneading, fashioning familiar shapes—a leg, a thigh, the soft and hidden skin beneath an arm. How her hands caressed and yearned. In my imagination, desire drove her mad, and I don't mean the desire for a particular face, a pair of certain hands, or the taste of another person's mouth, though that might have been there, too.

Let's say she once followed a woman with wavy black hair down a sidewalk in town. Trailed her inside a store that sold bolts of cloth, stood watching while the woman filled a paper bag with silver needles. How would it be, she wondered, to count the lines beside the woman's eyes with her fingers?

In my imagination, desire drove her mad, and I don't mean the desire for a particular face, certain hands, or the taste of another person's mouth, though that might have been there, too.

To memorize her face with touch? Later, when she bought something—a paper tape measure she didn't need—the air where the woman had stood had the sweet scent of roses. Desire had so many names she turned over and over in her mouth. The untied lace of a boot. The sigh of a dress falling against the floorboards. The moon's muted light. She longed to gather up all the names she found for desire and swallow them whole. No matter how cold the night, she kicked her legs out from the covers and let her skin drink air. There was no satiation. The room whispered secrets, and darkness gathered in the middle of her chest.

■ ■ ■

In the months before my cousin Greg killed himself, I'd been traveling in India with my then-lover. We made our way south from Nepal through Varanasi, west through Bihar, Utter Pradesh, Haryana, and Rajasthan. On the surface of things at least, India was shockingly immediate. Evidence of the body was everywhere. At every turn, hands touched us, asking us to rent rooms, to change money, to buy hashish. Men defecated at the feet of temple gods. Inside a stall women crouched, butchering a goat, the scent of blood rising in the stifling heat of summer. The dead were unconcealed, floating past us on the Ganges, lying spread-eagled in the river behind the Taj Mahal. Mourners painted their palms red and lit incense that choked the air with sweetness. When George and I got back to the United States, everything that had been so blatant in India resumed its secrecy. Muzak floated along the aisles of enormous grocery stores. Interstates were jammed with cars, their windows rolled up.

I'd been home a couple of weeks when I talked on the phone with my mother, who told me my cousin had died and that a funeral had been held a few days before. What happened, I wanted to know? I remembered Greg the last time I'd seen him. I'd been visiting the trailer where he lived. His mother, mine and another aunt sat in the kitchen smoking Winston's, everyone ignoring the music booming from a record player in Greg's room. Sadness seemed to ooze out of him as he paced the kitchen, his black eyes damp and red, his curly hair raked back from his forehead. He stood by the counter, his shit-kicker boots tapping to out an old Aerosmith song, his laughter nervous. He was the definition of wild, and I thought of the stories I'd heard about him—out of work at the mines, holding up a train, on speed, fathering a baby.

Later, when I drove back to Eastern Kentucky to visit, no one mentioned the word *suicide*. My mother and my aunt, Greg's mother, referred obliquely to something that had occurred, a something seemingly outside themselves. *When that happened to Greg*, they said when the subject of death came up. What I gathered is that he'd shot himself in his bedroom. Another time when I visited my aunt's trailer, I used the bathroom in the bedroom that had been Greg's, and I studied the floor and the paneled walls, looking for unwashable bloodstains left from gunshot. Nothing was there. Death had happened, but it had been folded into a tiny secret and hidden inside a drawer no one would open again.

■ ■ ■

In a long-ago writing class at Upward Bound, a motivational summer program for high schoolers, students described secrets using only immediate, sensory details. I spent my time getting to know as many of the students as I could—talking to them at lunch, asking to see their projects, checking on them if anything seemed amiss. From that writing class, I remember a description of a mouth hidden by a hand. A stretch of loamy soil, smoothed flat with a branch. Clouds obliterating the sun. The next part of the exercise was writing a page about releasing the secret. What did the mouth say when the hand was pulled away? Was the sunlight unadulterated happiness, or something else? Our chairs pushed into a circle, we wrote quietly and I occasionally looked up, studying them.

To one side of the circle was a girl I remember as big all over. She wore boxy, knee-length dresses, had large hands, long brown hair gathered in a big tangle on top of her head. The program was six weeks long, and during the weeks so far, the girl had sat by herself at lunch and underneath a tree during outdoor activities, arms circling her knees. During the group writing activity, she stared at the window, its long panes of dusty glass. Her lips moved and she wrote a word or two, chewed at the end of a pencil. At lunch that day, I made a point of inviting myself to sit with her, asked to hear what she'd written about. I don't remember if she revealed her secret then, or if it became obvious to all of us as the summer passed.

Her dress began to seem less boxy. It stretched across a stomach that grew more ample, and what had seemed like voluminous silences began to make sense. She was pregnant, seven, eight months along, and the pregnancy was a secret she'd kept not just from us, but from herself. She told the program coordinator she had not known she was pregnant— that she didn't know how she'd conceived, not when or where. As I remember it, the piece she'd written that day in the class went: *a secret is a whole world inside me, keeping itself as quiet as it can.* Her belly had grown larger and larger until it made itself known. Who was the father? We guessed at it, the secret she never told.

■ ■ ■

In Charlotte Bronte's *Jane Eyre,* the secret in the attic of Rochester's mansion is a "savage" of furrowed brow, black eyebrows, bloodshot eyes, reminiscent of "the foul German spectre—the Vampyre." The secret is a madwoman, mad, they say, because of a family lineage of mental illness, mad because of her dark, suspect race, mad because of her passionate (and unruly) Jamaican blood brought to live in the wild, desolate moors of England. Bertha Mason stands beside Jane's bed at night, laughing demonically, "a goblin-laugh," before she enters Rochester's room and sets fire to his bed curtains.

I read Bronte's novel many times as I was growing up, feeling the suppressed passion that Jane feels—the longing for recognition, love, touch—and the enormous power of the fire inside a woman's heart. I longed to look into Bertha Mason's face and make my own judgments about what savagery was, what madness looked like. I got that chance, later, when I read Jean Rhys's *Wide Sargasso Sea*. That novel was rich with the overpowering scent of flowers from the island of Antoinette's childhood, the scent of sex and power. Antoinette becomes Bertha, mourns her own passion hidden away in a room, transformed into madness. Secrecy becomes rage, and rage becomes fire as Bertha looks at Jane's wedding dress on the floor, dreaming it into flames.

■ ■ ■

Two years after our world travels, my lover fell in love with a beautiful woman who grew perennials in the greenhouse where he worked. He nose-dived away from our relationship, neither of us talking about the whys and hows. I blamed myself for the demise of things, since by then a small, nesting creature had taken up residence in my chest. Heaviness filled my hands and feet with a sludge I resisted as I tried to carry on with my life, but some days I couldn't stop crying. I was drowning in depression even before George fell out of love with me, and after he left I ended up for two weeks in a rehab center, the closest thing to emergency care my social worker/counselor could find for me on short notice. I played poker and watched *Rambo* movies in the break room with street people and heroin addicts. Then I checked myself out.

I was so lonely I wanted to die, but I took up the reins of my life again, furtively and with so much discomfort I seemed to be inside another body. On a cold night I cranked up a kerosene heater, went to make tea, returning to a room full of pale grey ash from the heater. Another night, as I talked at length on the phone, a soft thud resounded outside the kitchen window, and I looked up to see a huge black snake wrapped around the branch of a tree, swinging itself back and forth, back and forth against the window glass. The world was full of signs and dark wonders, but I couldn't read any of them. I lit candles every second day at an altar for the Sacred Heart at a Catholic Church in town. I prayed fervently, as if the world were a sealed box with the answers I needed, if only I could discover the key, but there was no key.

The world was full of signs and dark wonders, but I couldn't ready any of them...I prayed fervently, as if the world were a sealed box with the answers I needed, if only I could discover the key, but there was no key.

I had swallowed it and it lay at the bottom of my heart, turning and turning, releasing sorrow into my blood. I kept my lover's photograph taped to the refrigerator, lined up a pair of his old shoes next to the door.

One afternoon in town, I ordered fast food. I sat in my pickup with my plate of chicken livers and cole slaw in an alleyway behind a bookstore, devouring the food as if my life depended on it, until someone I knew walked by and saw me. He waved at me, a sign of friendship, and started toward my truck. I stepped on the accelerator, frightened that the secret of my sorrow had been discovered and thus might vanish like so much else had.

■ ■ ■

A child's rhyme: *one is for sorrow, two for joy, three for a girl, four for a boy, five for silver, six for god, seven for a secret, never to be told.* As far as I know, Stella's secret life in an upstairs room was never really told, except in rumors and offhand references I picked up and stored away over the years. Stella: the odd-turned, mad, contrary woman. I will never know for sure why she spent her life locked away. Mental illness never diagnosed. Such illnesses seen as mysterious signs from God, or from the devil. And if not mental illness, something else. A choice about love or belief. Or something simpler, but no less powerful. A woman full of so much power, so much radiance, it had to be contained somewhere. Perhaps, even, Stella contained herself in that room, unwilling to share who she was and what she felt with a world she couldn't tolerate. I will never know.

What I do know is that I come from generations of secrets. An aunt suffered from seizures and visions. I remember her lying down in the afternoon—long naps with the covers pulled over her head in the heat of the day. Another cousin spent time in rehab, for what I'm not sure. She, too, became a suicide no one talked about. Silences were huge and deafening, and there were smaller ones, more hushed secrets. Curtains drawn. Doors locked. Contents of drawers and envelopes taken out when I'd visit, secrets discussed one by one. This man who left this woman. This hurt. That one. Suffering to snack on, to live with, day by day by day.

■ ■ ■

Secrets should never be told.

Except I have told them, have opened the drawers, read the letters, asked the questions. I've told the truth, at least my version of it. As a memoirist, I believe that reaching far inside, turning truths over and over in my own two hands, translating them onto paper, is as close as I can get to real faith. And by reaching far inside, I have come upon my understanding of the truths of others. Aunts. Mother. God, even. Some days, I think I know why Stella was locked away from the world. Other days, my words are only careful guesses that, I hope, honor what really happened, when.

My own truth is that I've spent over twenty years, off and on, seeking the professional services of counselors. I've opened my mouth and taken Communion, both the wafer of the Lord and the medications I have hoped will pull me back up from the dark waters of myself. I've prayed in grand cathedrals and in the parking lots of little churches I've passed on road trips, ones closed on a Thursday afternoon. I've walked in graveyards and knelt beside markers where names and dates have long been illegible. I've hiked deserts and sat by the ocean, watching the waves go in, out. I've sought the consolation of everything from candles for the Blessed Mother that I light on my desk each morning to chants I listen to each night before I go to sleep. *Om Namah Shivaya.* I have bowed down to the truths as I come to know them.

Memoir is not a ripping away of the comfort that can be secrecy. Secrecy is the security of those closed curtains mid-day. It is the darkness that holds us on a night that feels like it will never end. It is the unsaid, held inside our cupped hands.

Memoir is a difficult act. It is speaking. Speaking up. Speaking out loud. Memoir hurts, but it does not dishonor, nor does it disown. It may renounce the cruelties of one's past, at the same time that it hopes beyond hope that there may be resolution, if not restitution. It speaks toward the truth, although it may never, ever, uncover the deepest part of what

is hidden. Maybe it's a song. The sound: *hush, hush, hush.*
Each tone, every *h*, transforms as it leaves the mouth. *Hush*
becomes *here. Here* becomes an invitation.

The mangy bird that has never been caught comes to
perch on our palms. We listen to what it has to tell us, and
then, perhaps, we set it free.

■ ■ ■

I have vivid dreams, many of them about houses. Houses
in Kentucky, North Carolina, Virginia. All the places I've
lived and written about in order to come a little closer to
uncovering the secrets of my life. I dream a small brown house
and the creosote bridge across a creek. I dream the house on a
lake where I lived alone for almost ten years, the path I walked
down to a dock where I leapt into the warm Georgia waters. I
dream kitchens, attics, a bedroom with a large stone fireplace.
I dream the dull red shine of a tile floor. A beat-up screen door
opens to a sun room where I used to sit with my granny at
breakfast. I don't think I've ever dreamed about Stella's house,
though writing scenes in memoir is a kind of dream.

In one such scene there's tall summer grass, unmowed
until you reach the yard. The speckled orange lilies called flags
are growing to one side of the house, and on the other side is a
gate no one needs. A garden reaching farther than I know how
to write. Instead I write myself walking up front steps, across a
small front porch. I could sit awhile if I wanted—here, or here
or here. The chairs on the porch are inviting, but tentative in
a way I can't describe. Metal chairs, their green paint peeling,
and thick spiderwebs in the porch eaves. Then there's the
small sound of a bell and a voice.

Stella, the voice calls, and it might be mine. A screenless
window is open, yellowed lace curtains blowing outside. After

time passes and I write some more, I am not sure if this scene is a painting or nothing more than a careful summoning against secrets. *Stella*, I call again, and I wait. ■

WILDFLOWERS

The first writing class told us not
what we should but what we shouldn't,
at least not until we outlived our excesses.
What was proscribed: dreams, grandparents
no doubt, ideas, our first beer, pets
dead or otherwise. In other words,
most of what most of us knew well
and well enough to love. Leaving us
to apprentice on other stuff—the sky at night,
the smaller losses, the backwoods where grow
the many wildflowers of North America
whose names, to this day, I still can't tell you.

KURT OLSSON

POEM

You tell it
knowing in telling it
you'll get it wrong
put the stress
in the wrong place
miss the pothole in the shallows
which is why
you must tell it
again knowing
you're sure
to make a wrong
exit in the same place
or more likely
some new screw up
so you keep telling
and telling it until
if you're lucky
the missteps become
the telling it
and you can stop.

KURT OLSSON

A QUIET VOICE

In a world of bluster and pyrotechnics,
of rage at injustice increasingly diplomatic,
a quiet voice can be disarming, describing
the large black eyes of a tufted titmouse,
its stern gaze and poise at the feeder. Note how—
in a quiet voice's attempt to reconcile a concept
as old fashioned as beauty with the anguish
the rest of us feel when loggers begin—there is,
despite the outcomes we know are inevitable,
a small measure of comfort, even consoling.
And if he spends too much effort wading out
into streams whose aquifers are under threat,
we understand, or at least believe, there is
defiance in how he bends to mossy stones,
studying the roots of sycamores along the bank,
seeming to relish the cold against his palms.
Surely we could learn from him a skepticism
masquerading as acceptance, a bitterness
made more deviant than most imagine by how
he reaches nonchalantly for pond side reeds
while letting their lengths slide through his grasp.
Might he know more forcefully how innocence
disrupts nations and movements; weakens,
by its presence, the plans of the strong; reminds
the spiteful that theirs is a kingdom where
nothing takes root but stones? If he does,
he doesn't say, and his not saying also seems
to be a voice, an even lower depth that might
be tactful, shrewd, or merely patient. Now he
speaks of moonlight mirrored in the dog's bowl,
of the owl on the barn roof stately as ever.

His might be a hymn only certain ears hear:
oak twig leafing out, persimmon turning red,
lifted-up straw settling farther, then father away.

JEFF HARDIN

WHEN IT ROLLS IN ITS BED

there's a child waist deep,
 there's a woman clinging
  to a tree, there's a dinghy
on what used to be a street in
Tennessee, fishing bodies. See the

man on a rooftop? The river breathes, sweeps
 us up against the guardrail of belief we
  might be spared. I open up the app for news of

forests that repair their sooty lungs. Of seas that world
 a surfeit of pearled oysters, but knee-deep, the wires like

electric eels, I wade through the events linked to collective
   deeds that leave us slogging

through the mud and caked debris, asking *please!*

BOOK REVIEWS

Robert Gipe. *Pop: An Illustrated Novel.* Athens, Oh.: Ohio University Press, 2021. 331 pages. Hardcover. $28.95.

Reviewed by Donna M. Crow

Toni Morrison once noted that William Faulkner possessed a "refusal-to-look-away approach in his writing," and over the course of three illustrated novels, Robert Gipe has found himself in similar territory with his confrontation of Appalachia's scars. Whether they be the corporate and political lies that have polarized and exploited Appalachians, or the more personal, self-created themes  of inequity caused by racism, misogyny and class, Gipe addresses them head-on. *Pop* is the latest and final installment of Robert Gipe's imaginatively illustrated trilogy which includes *Trampoline* (2015) and *Weedeater* (2018), both of which feature Dawn Jewell as their protagonist. In *Pop*, Dawn is joined by two other main characters—Nicolette and Uncle Hubert—and together their stories represent the voices of a whole town.

To say Gipe gets into the heads of his characters is an

understatement. It's more like Dawn Jewell has invited everyone she knew into the author's brain and they ran amok, leaving Gipe with nothing else to do but corral them into chapters like the wild ponies they are and listen closely to what they have to say. "Writing by ear," as Gipe himself calls it, denotes that the Jewell family refuses to let outsiders tell their story for them. Instead, struggling for control over their own lives, they forge a path of their own, leaving the author to hold on for dear life, write his heart out and draw what he sees.

Pop begins with a prologue by Dawn: "Me and my daughter [Nicolette Bilson] and our uncle Hubert [Jewell] are here to tell how we got on with our business on Long Ridge in the year 2016, twelve years after my mother died." Dawn warns us it is a hard story, a generational story full of emotional triggers. "I was twenty-one when Momma got caught up in a den of pillshooters and they shot her up with OxyContin and killed her in the heat of a July night and dumped her body under a oak tree by the river behind the floodwall. Those did that were her friends, my friends too." Although Dawn is still only thirty-two, she says, "I feel like I've been telling my story for a thousand years" and is "… tired down to my bones." With *Pop*, seventeen-year-old Nicolette has inherited the fortitude to carry the Jewell family toward the light. As Dawn says, "a sparkle and lilt marks [Nicolette] in the time of me telling you this." The Jewell family is a hard-shelled, resilient bunch.

This is a hard story, deeply layered and clever, right down to the name of the county in which the Jewell family lives, Canard, defined as an unfounded rumor or story. Though the things that happen in Gipe's Canard County ring true, the characters must always decipher reality from the corporate and political lies they've been told. While every Appalachian experience is not that of the Jewell family, true Appalachians recognize the Jewells and their struggle to stay afloat in a world that means to drown them.

Although readers of *Trampoline* and *Weedeater* know Uncle Hubert as an outlaw, prone to anything from bootlegging to money laundering to hiding dead bodies, in *Pop* he has evolved into the (somewhat) less shady self-proclaimed patriarch-protector of the Jewell family. He does what he must to protect his great niece Nicolette from his no-good nephew Colbert, who sexually assaults her, but still we later hear Hubert say, "I had tried to tell that boy these women don't put up with stuff like they used to" and that Colbert stands for "the way things used to be." With lines like this, Gipe gifts us with his ability to expose the truth without authorial interference. He lets his characters act, react, get into trouble, take the law into their own hands, and speak for themselves, whether he might agree with them or not.

Gipe's Faulknerian-like stream-of-consciousness writing style, filled with details, descriptions and actions, can backfill a story with an economy of words. In a two-page monologue that comes in the book's final section, Hubert reconciles his past and present, tells us he loved a trans woman named Tildy, who has just died. Then he sits "alone with the many chickens that had come home to roost for old Hubert," and recites a list of the sins of his past as posted on Facebook by an angry (although forgiven) Dawn. These sins include housefires, stolen liquor, and cheating, among other offenses. This one monologue provides the reader with Hubert's whole backstory from the first two books.

Any critical analysis of Gipe's literary work could spend hours on the adroit weaving of his innovative illustrations into text. Cunningly, his characters rise in his mind, leap out of their own words into images and land in the middle of a paragraph as if they have waited too long to tell their story. Days could be spent on characterization, the way he brings a whole passel of folks to bare unapologetically the ugliest parts of their personalities while somehow exposing their vulnerability. Gipe's skillful mastery of language is another strength that will be written about and spoken of for years to come in sentences that will no doubt include Faulkner and James Still. His use of authentic voices, diction and syntax are spot on. His metaphors and similes are as fresh as an unused Kleenex, all grounded in a sense of place so hard and beautiful it is worth fighting over. And fight these characters do, against the exploitations from without and from within.

From mountaintop removal coal mining to chemical plant spills to the opioid epidemic, Gipe doesn't miss a hitch. A complicated lot, the residents of Canard County run the gambit from an "old white guy" to a transgender woman to gay teenagers and everyone in between. This author brings to the conversation just about every issue that plagues America today, but not without a good measure of old-fashioned Appalachian culture and tradition. From talk of "haints" and witches, making sorghum molasses, and old-fashioned stack cake and skillet cornbread, to organizing an uprising over the Internet or taking over a Hollywood movie plot filmed in the region, Gipe schools us in the complexity and resilience of what it is to be a contemporary Appalachian. Whether Robert Gipe set out to write the quintessential Appalachian novel or not, he most certainly has done so. ∎

EVEN YEARS LATER

I always know their flower faces,
although I do not always remember their names

would recognize them by their handwriting

can recall intimate details they once scrawled
in black ink on pages of spiral-bound notebooks

doodles, drawings, designs inscribed vertically
to the left of the pink line before the edges tatter

and corners fray. Pages torn out, impressions
left behind like ghost words too haunted to share

with a teacher.

B. ELIZABETH BECK

CONTRIBUTORS

Zachary Bartles was raised in the Shenandoah Valley of West Virginia. He now lives in East Texas with his wife, where he is a stay-at-home father to their daughter.

B. Elizabeth Beck is a writer, artist, and teacher who is the author of the *Summer Tour Trilogy.* Founder of the Teen Howl Poetry Series and the award-winning Leestown OUTLOUD Poets, Beck also volunteers her time teaching writing workshops. Her collections of poems include: *Mama Tried* (forthcoming from Broadstone Books in 2022), *Painted Daydreams: Collection of Ekphrastic Poems* (Accents Publishing 2018), *Interiors* (Finishing Line Press 2011), *insignificant white girl* (Evening Street Press 2011).

Donna M. Crow, a resident of Estill County, Kentucky, is the third generation to live on her family farm. She writes fiction, creative nonfiction, and poetry. Her work has appeared previously in *Appalachian Review, Still: The Journal, Now and Then, The Minnetonka Review, The Louisville Review, Blue Lyra Review* and other publications. She received her MFA in Creative Nonfiction from Spalding University.

Sarah Grace Goolden is a recent graduate of University of North Carolina at Greensboro and is now attending American University for her MFA in Creative Writing. She is the poetry editor for *FOLIO* magazine and the previous opinion editor of *The Carolinian.* Goolden has worked as a high school English teacher and hopes to return after graduation to instill the same passion for literature that her teachers have gifted her. Her work has been published or is forthcoming in *Inside The Bell Jar, The Coraddi, The Dillydoun* Review and *Defunkt Magazine.*

Megan Gower graduated from Appalachian State University with her B.A. in English with concentrations in both creative writing and professional writing. She attended the Columbia Publishing Course and worked in New York publishing before deciding to return to North Carolina to acquire her graduate degree in poetry at the

University of North Carolina at Greensboro. She currently teaches undergraduate writing and literature courses as a lecturer at UNCG.

Jeff Hardin is the author of six collections of poetry: *Fall Sanctuary* (Nicholas Roerich Prize); *Notes for a Praise Book* (Jacar Press Book Award); *Restoring the Narrative* (Donald Justice Prize); *Small Revolution; No Other Kind of World* (X. J. Kennedy Prize), and A *Clearing Space in the Middle of Being. The New Republic, The Hudson Review, The Southern Review, Southwest Review, North American Review, The Gettysburg Review, Poetry Northwest, Hotel Amerika,* and *Southern Poetry Review* have published his poems. He teaches at Columbia State Community College in Columbia, Tennessee.

Kathleen Hellen's credits include two chapbooks, *The Girl Who Loved Mothra* and *Pentimento*, and her award-winning collection *Umberto's Night*. Her work has appeared in *Ascent, Barrow Street, The Carolina Quarterly, Colorado Review, Four Way Review, Grist, jubilat, New American Writing, New Letters, North American Review, Prairie Schooner, Puerto del Sol, The Rumpus, Sewanee Review, Spoon River Poetry Review, Subtropics, The Sycamore Review, Verse Daily,* and *West Branch*, among others. Hellen's latest poetry collection is *The Only Country Was the Color of My Skin.*

Ron Houchin has published eight books of poetry, including *Talking to Shadows, The Man Who Saws Us in Half, Museum Crows,* and *Planet of the Best Love Songs.* His work has appeared in the *Birmingham Poetry Review, Five Points, Poetry Northwest, the Southwest Review,* and many other publications. A retired schoolteacher, he lives on the banks of the Ohio River across from Huntington, West Virginia, where he grew up.

Dan Leach has published poetry and short fiction in *Copper Nickel, The New Orleans Review,* and *The Sun.* He lives in South Carolina and teaches English at a small liberal arts university. He holds an MFA from Warren Wilson.

Karen Salyer McElmurray earned an MFA from the University of Virginia, an MA in Creative Writing from Hollins University, and a PhD from the University of Georgia. Her work has received numerous awards, including grants from the National Endowment for the Arts. She has published multiple fiction and creative nonfiction books including *Surrendered Child* and *Motel of the Stars.* An essay collection, *Voice Lessons,* was released by Iris Press in June 2021.

Kurt Olsson has published two collections of poetry, the most recent being *Burning Down Disneyland* (Gunpowder Press, 2017), selected by Thomas Lux as the winner of the Barry Spacks Poetry Prize. Olsson's poetry has recently appeared or is forthcoming in *SLANT, Another Chicago Magazine, North Dakota Quarterly, Paterson Literary Review,* and *Cincinnati Review.*

John Picard is a native of Washington, D.C. living in North Carolina. He received his MFA from the University of North Carolina at Greensboro. He has published fiction and nonfiction in *The Iowa Review, Narrative Magazine, Gettysburg Review, New England Review, Alaska Quarterly Review,* and elsewhere. A collection of his stories, *Little Lives,* was published by Main Street Rag. More information can be found at johnmpicard.com.

John Saad lives and works in Birmingham, Alabama. His poetry has most recently appeared in *The Pinch, Raleigh Review, Terrain.org,* and *Poetry South.* His chapbook, *Longleaf,* was the winner of the Hopper Poetry Prize and was published in 2017 through Green Writers Press in Vermont. Besides poetry, Saad manages his family's 200-acre forestland in Alabama's Black Belt region. He is currently working to certify this land with national and state stewardship programs that are committed to producing healthier forests among private forest landowners.

Dana Shavin's work has appeared in *Oxford American, The Sun, Fourth Genre, Alaska Quarterly Review,* and others, and her essay "This Strange Ballet" is forthcoming from *Garden and Gun.* She has been a columnist for the *Chattanooga Times Free Press* since 2002, and her memoir, *The Body Tourist,* was published by Little Feather books in 2014. Shavin's work has been nominated for a Pushcart Prize and for inclusion in *Best American Essays.*

Lauren Smothers has published poems and photography in *storySouth, Juke Joint,* and elsewhere. A graduate of the MFA program at the University of North Carolina at Greensboro, she is the founder and manager of Light Trap Books, an independent bookstore located in the heart of downtown, Jackson, Tennessee.

Originally from Washington, D.C., **Maura Way** lives in North Carolina, by way of Boise, Idaho. Her work has previously appeared in *The Chattahoochee Review, Folio, Yemassee,* and *Poet Lore,* among other publications. *Another Bungalow,* her debut collection, was released by Press 53 in 2017. She has been a schoolteacher for over twenty years, most recently at New Garden Friends School in Greensboro.

William Kelley Woolfitt's poems, short stories, and essays have appeared in *AGNI, Blackbird, Image, Tin House, The Threepenny Review, The Gettysburg Review,* and elsewhere. He is the author of three poetry collections: *Beauty Strip* (Texas Review Press, 2014), *Charles of the Desert* (Paraclete Press, 2016), and *Spring Up Everlasting* (Mercer University Press, 2020).

Kelly Zanotti is a writer living and mothering in southwestern Virginia. Her work has appeared in *River Teeth, the Virginia Literary Review, Volume, the Hollins Critic,* and elsewhere. Her poetry has been twice nominated for the AWP Intro Journals Prize and has been longlisted for the Poetry Society's National Poetry Competition. She holds an MFA from Hollins University.

www.ingramcontent.com/pod-product-compliance
Lightning Source LLC
Chambersburg PA
CBHW070603180626
46817CB00005B/1981